CW00369965

Ultimate Aussie
Insults
& Jokes

SUMMIT PRESS

950 Stud Road, Rowville
Victoria 3174 Australia
Phone: +61 3 8756 5500
Fax: +61 3 8756 5588

First published 2003

© Summit Press

All rights reserved

Compiled by Sonya Plowman
Cartoons by Geoff Hocking
Designed by SBR Productions Olinda Victoria

Printed in Australia by Griffin Press

The National Library of Australia Cataloguing-in-Publication data:
Ultimate Aussie Insults and Jokes.

ISBN 1 86503 742 7.

1. Australian wit and humor. 2. Invective - Australia. I. Hocking,
Geoff, 1947- . II. Plowman, Sonya, 1972- .

A828.02

Ultimate Aussie
Insults
& Jokes

Compiled by Sonya Plowman
Cartoons by Geoff Hocking

SUMMIT
PRESS

Contents

Introduction

Aussies like nothing better than to take the piss out of someone, and if they can do it with a light-hearted insult while they're at it, all the better. To ensure maximum offensiveness when you next feel like insulting someone, here's a selection of very politically incorrect slights, put-downs and jokes to choose from. Whether you want to rib your mate next door, pick on the Irish bloke down the street or confuse the dumb blonde walking past your driveway, you're bound to find the following useful.

Sonya Plowman

To the Completely Stupid

Insults

You couldn't organise a piss-up in a brewery.

★★★

You couldn't hit a dead bull's bum with a tin can.

★★★

Not all your dogs are barking.

★★★

There's no Vegemite on your sandwich.

★★★

Not all your chooks are clucking.

★★★

If bullshit were music, you'd have your own orchestra.

You're a few sprinkles short of a fairy-bread sandwich.

***

You're as thick as the dust on a public servant's out-tray.

***

You're a few sheep short in the top paddock.

***

You're not the full two bob.

***

Thinking isn't exactly your strong point, is it?

***

You're a few slices short of a loaf.

***

The closest you'll ever come to a brainstorm is a drizzle.

***

If bullshit were rubber, you'd fly to the moon.

I hear you changed your mind. So what did you do with the nappy?

★★★

Some people drink from the fountain of knowledge, but it seems that you gargled.

★★★

Not all your dingoes are in the yard.

★★★

Your lunchbox is missing a banana.

★★★

You're not playing with the full deck.

★★★

You're not the full packet of Tim Tams.

★★★

You're dippier than a Jatz cracker.

★★★

If clues were shoes, you'd be wearing thongs.

★★★

Are you normally this stupid or are you having a blonde moment?

★★★

You're not the full quid.

★★★

There might be space for a brain in your head if you cleared out some of the shit.

★★★

You're off with the fairies.

★★★

You wouldn't know if your arse was on fire!

★★★

You're naturally blonde, aren't you?

★★★

It seems you're suffering from diarrhoea of the mouth and constipation of the ideas.

★★★

I'd be better off down at the supermarket talking to the vegies.

★★★

If ignorance was a disability, you'd get the full pension.

★★★

I'd like to see things from your point of view, but I can't seem to get my head that far up my arse.

★★★

You wouldn't shout in a shark attack.

★★★

You're not worth a rat's arse.

★★★

You've got nothing between the ears except pixie breath.

★★★

You're going through life with your headlights on dim.

★★★

You're a lettuce leaf short of a salad.

★★★

You're as silly as a wet hen.

★★★

You're a few peanuts short of a jar of peanut butter.

★★★

You're a flamin' dingo!

★★★

You're so slow you couldn't get a job as a
speed hump.

★★★

You're so wet I could shoot ducks off you.

★★★

You're as thick as a brick.

★★★

You've only got one oar in the water.

★★★

You must have a mammoth brain to hold so much stupidity.

★★★

Is that a dick on your shoulders? Oh, sorry, it's just your head.

★★★

Yeah, I can see your point, but I still think you're full of shit.

★★★

Go ahead, tell them everything you know. It'll only take ten seconds.

★★★

It sounds like English, but I can't understand a word you're saying.

★★★

I wish I had a hearing-aid so I could switch you off.

★★★

You're a brick short of a load.

★★★

You're a patient short of a loony bin.

★★★

You're as bright as a two-watt bulb.

★★★

You couldn't run guts for a slow butcher.

★★★

You're a couple of pies short of a grand final.

★★★

You're so dense you drive uphill with the clutch slipping.

★★★

When God was handing out brains, you were out chewing your cud with the cows.

★★★

You're so stupid, you'd count the coconut sprinkles on a lamington.

★★★

Every time you open your mouth, some dickhead starts talking.

★★★

You're a few stubbies short of a six-pack.

★★★

You've got space to sell between your ears, but no one wants to buy it.

★★★

You haven't got all four paws on the mouse.

★★★

There's nothing wrong with having nothing to say – unless you insist on saying it.

★★★

Does your train of thought have a caboose?

★★★

You're a trifle short of custard.

★★★

I see you've set aside this special time to make a complete dickhead of yourself.

★★★

Do you talk bullshit all the time or only when you open your mouth?

★★★

How do you keep a dickhead in suspense?
Don't worry, I'll tell you later.

★★★

You think you're such a smart-arse. As usual, you're only half right.

★★★

You have an intellect rivalled only by the village idiot's dead-shit brother.

★★★

If you had an idea it would die of loneliness.

★★★

Your lift doesn't go all the way to the top floor.

★★★

If your brains were dynamite, you couldn't blow your hat off.

★★★

Your lights are on, but there's nobody home.

★★★

You've only got fifty cards in the deck.

★★★

You're short of numbers in the Upper House.

★★★

You're a snag short of a barbie.

★★★

When God was handing out brains, you were busy counting stones in the gravel.

★★★

You couldn't turn over a snag at a barbie.

★★★

You're three beers short of a shout.

★★★

If your brains were dynamite, you wouldn't have enough to part your hair.

★★★

You're a tinnie short of a slab.

★★★

You wouldn't know your arse from your elbow.

★★★

You wouldn't know whether it's Tuesday or Bourke Street.

★★★

You wouldn't know a sheep from your missus.

★★★

You're up the pole, mate.

★★★

You're so stupid, you ran out of fuel leaving the BP.

★★★

You're as bright as a kiddie's nightlight.

★★★

You're as quick as a corpse.

★★★

Don't let your mind wander – it's too small to be let out on its own.

★★★

You der!

★★★

I'll try being nicer if you'll try being smarter.

★★★

First of all you're an idiot. And second of all –
I think that's it.

***

You're all foam and no beer.

***

You're all hat and no cattle.

***

You couldn't pick out the colour white in a
snowstorm.

***

If your brains were dynamite, you couldn't
blow your eyebrows off.

***

You couldn't organise a fart in a baked beans
factory.

***

Are you always this stupid or are you making
a special effort today?

***

You couldn't organise a wet t-shirt competition
at Playboy headquarters.

***

You've got shit for brains.

If your brains were dynamite, you wouldn't have enough to blow your nose.

You're a ning-nong.

If your brains were elastic, they wouldn't make a set of garters for a one-legged budgie.

You're so stupid, you wouldn't know if a band was up you till you got the drum.

You couldn't run out of sight on a dark night.

You wouldn't know whether it's Queen Street or Christmas.

You're a ding-dong.

Watch out – if you pick your nose, your head will cave in.

★★★

You haven't got enough brains to give yourself a headache.

★★★

You haven't got enough sense to come in out of the rain.

★★★

You're a dropkick.

★★★

If your brains were shit, you wouldn't have enough to soil your tie.

★★★

If you were given a brain it would be lonely.

★★★

You're not firing on all six cylinders.

★★★

You're a mopoke.

★★★

You're an egg-salad sandwich short of a picnic.

★★★

You can see daylight through your ears.

★★★

Your roof's a shingle short.

★★★

You're a twit.

★★★

Your tree's short of foliage.

★★★

If you donated your brain to science, they'd give it back.

★★★

You're as slow as a paralysed turtle.

★★★

You're as silly as a tin of worms.

★★★

You're a droob.

★★★

You're all over the shop.

★★★

You wouldn't know if a bus was up you till the people got off.

★★★

You're as silly as a two-bob watch.

★★★

Your IQ is way below room temperature.

★★★

You're as slow as a wet week.

★★★

You wouldn't know if a train was up you till the whistle blew.

★★★

You've got the IQ of a green banana.

★★★

You're a brick short of a load.

★★★

You're a cough drop.

★★★

You're as silly as a solar-powered torch.

***

You're a bit slow off the mark.

***

You went to the race, but you forgot to leave the start line.

***

You're a Sally.

***

You're soft in the crumpet.

***

You're a drongo.

***

You've got a brain like a cow's udder.

***

You're ten cents short of a dollar.

***

You're a dingbat.

***

You're an umbrella short of a cocktail.

***

You're as thick as two planks.

★★★

You wouldn't know if a tram was up you till the conductor started checking your tickets.

★★★

You're a Wally.

★★★

You wouldn't know your arse from a hole in a flowerpot.

★★★

You're as thick as pig shit.

★★★

You're a dill.

★★★

You're so stupid, you sold the house to pay the mortgage.

★★★

You're so dumb, even blondes tell jokes about you.

★★★

You're so dumb, you couldn't find your arse if both of your hands were tied behind your back.

★★★

You'd have to get smarter just to be plain stupid.

★★★

You're as dumb as a Mallee root.

★★★

You've got the brains of a dunny brush.

★★★

You're dumber than a sackful of hammers.

★★★

I smell hair burning – you must be thinking too hard.

★★★

You're as smart as whitebait.

★★★

You're as sharp as the pointy ends of a footy.

If your brains were shit, you wouldn't need any toilet paper.

★★★

You're a galah.

★★★

If you had another brain, you could start a rock garden.

★★★

You're a gink.

★★★

You couldn't see the road to the dunny if it had red flags on it.

★★★

You're as dumb as koala poop.

★★★

You're a nong.

★★★

You couldn't catch a cold if you sat naked all night in an icy billabong.

★★★

You couldn't f*** a frog trotting.

★★★

You couldn't kick a hen off its nest.

***

You couldn't piss in a boot with the directions written on the tongue.

***

You're a goose.

***

You couldn't poke a sharp stick up a dead cat's arse.

***

You couldn't sell a statue to a pigeon.

***

You're a dingaling.

***

You'd wear a ski-jacket in Cairns.

***

You're as thick as Uluru.

***

You're not the full packet of Smarties.

***

You couldn't find your arse with both hands and a floodlight.

***

You're not the brightest crayon in the box.

***

Born at night, were you? Last night, I gather.

***

You're not the brightest bulb on the Christmas tree.

***

You're not the sharpest knife in the drawer.

***

You couldn't scratch your arse if you were holding a tiger.

***

If you put an axe in your head, it would take a few swings to break through the deadwood.

***

You're a dipstick.

***

You obviously come from the shallow end of the gene pool.

You're as slow as a holiday in Canberra.

Jokes

After muddling his way through most of the lengthy written instructions for the ATM, the customer eventually got stuck and walked over to a bank officer.

'Excuse me,' said the customer, 'but I was wondering if you could help me out.'

'Sure,' replied the teller, 'just go through that door.'

★★★

A Scotsman, an Italian and an Irishman are in a bar. They are having a good time and all agree that the bar is a cool place to hang out. Then the Scotsman says, 'Aye, this bar's alright, but where I come from, back in Glasgee, there's a better one. At MacDonnell's, ye buy a drink, ye buy another drink, and MacDonnell himself will buy ye third drink!' The others agree that MacDonnell's sounds like a good place.

Then the Italian says, 'Yeah, dat sounds like a nice bar, but where I come from, dere's a better one. In Roma, dere's dis place, Papa

Luigi's. At Papa Luigi's, you buy a drink, Papa
Luigi buys you a drink. You buy anudda drink,
Papa Luigi buys you anudda drink.'
Everyone agrees that Papa Luigi's sounds like
a great bar.
Then the Irishman says, 'You tink dat's great?
Where oi come from in Dublin, dere's dis
place called Murphy's. At Murphy's, dey boy
you your first drink, dey boy you your second
drink, den dey boy you your tird drink, and
den, after all dat, dey take you in de back and
get you laid!'
'Wow!' say the other two, full of jealousy.
'That's fantastic! Did that happen to you?'
'No,' says the Irish guy, 'but it happened to me
sister!'

★★★

A builder named Ben was rushed to the Royal
Melbourne Hospital one day, his foot wrapped
in bandages and bleeding profusely.
'What happened?' asked the doctor.
'Well,' began Ben, 'about fifteen years ago, I
began as a builder's apprentice in Bendigo,
and I –'
'Wait! Fifteen years ago? What about your
foot?'
'I'm getting to that, just hold on,' said Ben.
'Anyway, I was learning my trade under a
builder named Harry, and I was living in his

house. The night that I moved into his house, his gorgeous daughter Tamara came into my room wearing a skimpy, sexy nightgown. She said to me, "Is there anything I can do for you, Ben?" And I said, "No, thank you, Tamara, I have everything I need; I am fine." The next night she came back wearing that sexy little piece again, and had on this lovely perfume that made her smell like a blossoming rose. And she said, "Ben, is there anything at all I can do for you?"

And I said, "No, thank you kindly, Tamara, I have everything I need; I am fine."

The next night she came in completely starkers and asked me again, "Is there anything at all I can do for you, sweetest Ben?"

And I was a little embarrassed, but gently said to her, "Thanks very much, Tamara, but I have everything I need; I'm fine.'"

The doctor shifted impatiently and sighed in exasperation. 'Pray tell, Ben. What on Earth does this have to do with your foot?!'

Ben rolled his eyes and scowled. 'Well, this morning, I finally figured out what she meant, and I got so angry at myself that I threw down a hammer and busted my foot!'

It's the last day of the school year at the local high school and the principal is handing out Year 12 certificates – every student except one has passed their exams. The one who didn't pass is Alex, a popular guy whose only skill was sport – he was the best footballer in the district. Not only was he captain of the footy team, he was also a state champion. As the principal walks past Alex, the students begin to chant, 'Give Alex a chance! Give Alex a chance!'

The principal, worried that things might get ugly, and really just wanting a peaceful life, says, 'Okay, Alex. I'm going to ask you a simple question, and if you get it right I'll give you your certificate. What is the capital of Queensland?'

Alex thinks for a moment and answers, 'Uh, Cairns?'

The principal says, 'Sorry, Alex, that's wrong.'

The students begin to chant again, 'Give Alex a chance, give Alex a chance.'

The principal sighs and says, 'Okay, Alex, one more chance. What is the capital of Western Australia?'

Alex thinks for a second and then says, 'Kalgoorlie?'

The principal groans and says, 'Sorry Alex, that's wrong.'

The students begin the chant once more, 'Give

Alex a chance, give Alex a chance.'
The principal mutters under his breath and
decides to give the student just one more go.
'Okay, Alex, this really is your last chance.
What is the capital of Australia?'
Alex immediately answers, 'Canberra.'
The students chant, 'Give him another chance!'

★★★

Papa Bear and Baby Bear went into the
kitchen for breakfast one morning.
'Someone's eaten my porridge,' wailed Baby
Bear.
'And someone has eaten my porridge,'
grumbled Papa Bear.
'You bloody idiots!' yelled Mama Bear. 'I
haven't even made the damn stuff yet.'

★★★

A popular rock band began a world tour,
hoping to gain some new fans and sell
thousands of records. The band's first
destination was Scotland. As they had some
time to kill before their first gig, the drummer
and bass player went on a trip to Edinburgh.
They soon began arguing about how to
pronounce it.
'It's "Ed-in-burra",' said the bass player.
'No way, you pronounce it "Ed-in-berg",' said
the drummer.

To settle it once and for all they decided to ask a local. Stopping at a hamburger joint, they asked the girl behind the counter, 'Tell us, love, just how do you pronounce the name of this place?'

She looked at them strangely for a minute, then said very slowly and carefully, 'Mc-don-alds.'

★★★

Sherlock Holmes and Dr Watson went out hiking one long weekend. After stumbling upon a nice camping ground, they set up their tent, enjoyed a few beers and trundled off to their sleeping bags.

In the early hours, Sherlock awoke and urgently shook Watson from his slumber. 'Dear Watson!' he exclaimed, 'Look up at the sky and tell me what you see, my good man!'

Watson wearily replied, 'Why, Holmes, I can see a sky full of stars.'

Sherlock narrowed his eyes toward the Milky Way. 'I see, Watson. And what conclusions do you draw from this sky full of stars?'

Thinking that Sherlock was about to launch into a great sermon on the meaning of life, Watson decided to leap one step ahead of the great detective. Clearing his throat, he orated, 'Well, Holmes, in astronomical terms, the sky full of stars tells me that there are millions of galaxies, billions of planets, and, quite possibly, other life forms existing in the great yonder. In astrological terms, I think that Mercury is in retrograde, and we are entering a Libran phase. In theological terms, I can tell you that God is an all-knowing and powerful being and that we are but insignificant ants in this universe. In horological and meteorological terms, I can tell you that it is three-fifteen, and that we will enjoy a pleasantly warm and sunny day hiking tomorrow. Tell me, what conclusions do *you* draw from this sky full of stars, dear Holmes?' 'Watson, you fool!' sighed the super-sleuth. 'The sky full of stars tells me that someone has stolen our tent!'

★★★

One day Carl went out scuba diving. He was three metres below sea level when he noticed a guy at the same depth he was, but without any scuba gear. Carl went a further three metres down, and what do you know, the guy joined him a few minutes later. Carl was really puzzled by this, but continued further down yet another three metres. The guy caught up with him once again.

By this stage, Carl couldn't believe his eyes. He took out his waterproof blackboard and chalked on it, 'How on Earth are you able to stay under this deep without any scuba equipment?'

The guy snatched away the board and chalk, scribbled over what Carl had written, and scrawled, 'I'm drowning, you idiot!'

***

A geeky little fella walks into a bar and slips on a pile of dog poop in the doorway. Composing himself, he wipes his feet and walks over to the bar and orders a drink.

A few minutes later, a burly bikie walks into the bar and also slips on the pile of dog poop. After throwing about a few curses, he saunters up to the bar and orders a drink.

Smiling weakly, the geeky little fella says, 'Oh,

I just did that!'
So the bikie punched him.

★★★

Two truckies come to an underpass. The clearance sign says that all vehicles must measure a maximum of twelve foot. One of the blokes gets out of the cabin and measures the truck. It's fourteen foot.
'Bugger! We exceed the clearance maximum by two foot,' he exclaims. 'We're going to have to back up and go a different route.'
'What are you talking about, mate?' says the other truckie revving the engine, 'There's no coppers around. Who's going to know that we drove under the flamin' bridge?'

★★★

The new secretary spends her first week on the job spilling coffee over important documents, announcing the wrong company name when answering the telephone, and awkwardly chicken-pecking letters out on the keyboard with just two fingers.
On Friday afternoon, her boss sighs, 'Listen, love. I think it's best if you don't bother coming on Monday.'
Delighted, the new secretary replies, 'Wow, thanks! I'll see you Tuesday, then.'

★★★

A snail crawls into a bar just on closing time.
He knocks on the door until the barman
finally opens the door, and looks around.
When he sees the snail he says, 'Go away.
We're closed, and besides, we don't serve
snails here.' He then slams the door in the
snail's face. The snail again pounds on the
door until the bartender gets so frustrated that
he opens the door and kicks the snail away.
A year later as the bartender is closing up for
the night, he hears a pounding on the door.
He opens the door, and who is there but the
same snail from a year previous. The snail
looks up and says, 'What did you do that for?'

A man walks into a psychiatrist's office and
says, 'Doctor, I need your help. I think I'm
a dog.'
The psychiatrist replies, 'Well get up on the
couch and we'll talk about it.'
The guy says, 'Can't. I'm not allowed on
the couch.'

★★★

To the Utterly Psycho

Insults

You've been touched in the head, and I think it was with a jackhammer.

★★★

You're as nutty as a date loaf.

★★★

You're off your 'nana.

★★★

You haven't lost the plot, you've lost the whole library.

★★★

You're loopier than an onion ring.

★★★

You're bonkers.

★★★

Don't drop your bundle!

★★★

You're berko.

★★★

You've got some palings off the fence.

★★★

You've got white ants in the woodwork.

★★★

You've got kangaroos loose in your top paddock.

★★★

You're as mad as a gumtree full of galahs.

★★★

You've got nits in the network.

★★★

You're wacko.

★★★

Your cheese has slid off its cracker.

★★★

You're all over the shop.

★★★

You're off your pannikin.

★★★

You're off your rocker.

★★★

You fell off the merry-go-round and they're not letting you back on.

★★★

You're round the twist.

★★★

Don't chuck a wobbly!

★★★

You're sillier than a pork chop.

★★★

You're as mad as a two-bob watch.

★★★

You've left your muzzle at home.

★★★

You're as mad as a hatter.

★★★

You're up the pole.

★★★

Your common sense has gone AWOL and
she's not coming back.

★★★

You're as mad as a cut snake.

★★★

You're as barmy as a bandicoot.

★★★

You're bats.

★★★

Don't do your lolly!

★★★

You've got several screws loose, and your nuts
are all over the place.

★★★

You've got bats in your belfry.

★★★

You spit more chips than the Birdseye factory.

★★★

You're off your kadoova.

★★★

Your ladder is missing a few rungs.

★★★

You're as testy as a bull in a cowshed.

★★★

Don't do your block!

★★★

You'd be mates with Norman Bates.

★★★

You're as wound up as a 1000-day clock.

★★★

There's mould in your fridge and you're cooking it for dinner.

★★★

You're touched.

★★★

You're a basket case.

★★★

You're as mad as a meat axe.

★★★

You're troppo.

★★★

Your budgie's flown out of the cage.

★★★

You're not the full quid.

★★★

Your driveway doesn't quite reach the carport.

★★★

You're all over the place like a dog's breakfast.

★★★

You're as bent as a scrub tick.

★★★

Jokes

Out on the beat one night, a policeman came across a bruised and bloodied young man on the footpath.

'Mate, what happened? Can you describe the person who beat you up?'

'Of course,' said the young bloke, spitting out a few teeth. 'In fact, that's exactly what I was doing when the crazy son of a bitch slugged me.'

★★★

Two middle-aged blokes are sitting in a pub enjoying a few brews. In saunters a young punk with a crazy coloured mohawk. The two blokes smirk at one another and the punk notices their look. Strutting up to their bar stools, he snarls, 'Oi! Do you old farts have some sort of a problem? What do you think you're looking at, hey?'

One of the men clears his throat and says, 'Er ... no, mate. We don't have a problem. In fact, I think that you might be my son.'

'Oh yeah?' says the punk suspiciously, 'And what makes you think that?'
'About 22 years ago, I had sex with a parrot that looked just like you.'

***

Little Billy was a very bad boy who wanted a bike more than anything else in the world. His mother said he could only have one if he started behaving himself, which he promised to do. He tried as hard as he could, but his naughty habits were well entrenched and he kept on getting into trouble. His mother could see that he was trying to be good, so she suggested that he write a letter to Jesus as it might make it easier for him to behave.
Little Billy went to his room and began to write a letter.
'Dear Jesus,' he began, 'I promise to behave for the rest of my life if you give me a bike.'
Realising that he couldn't keep this promise, he started again. 'Dear Jesus, if you give me a bike, I'll be good for a month.'
Thinking for a second, Billy realised that even that promise would be broken, so he screwed up the paper.
Running into his parents' bedroom, he removed his mum's statue of the Holy Mother, put it in a shoebox, and hid it in his desk drawer.

He started on a new sheet of paper. 'Dear Jesus, if you ever want to see your mother again ...'

★★★

A married couple were out on the golfing green one afternoon. At the eighth hole, the man suddenly keels over, stone-cold dead. His wife throws him over her shoulder and heads back toward the country club.

Once she's there, an ambulance is called and they attempt to revive her husband. The other club members marvel at her bravery, and ask how did she manage to carry her dead husband all the way from the eighth hole. Nonplussed, the woman replies, 'Oh, carrying him across the green wasn't the hard bit. But picking him up and putting him down after each shot got pretty tiring.'

★★★

Ted was a carpenter and he had been brazenly working on the circular saw whilst drinking a cup of coffee. Being a little clumsy, Ted dropped his cup right onto the redwood that he'd been crafting. As he tried to save the cup, his hands connected with the circular saw and all ten fingers were sliced clean from his hand. Running out of his workshop onto the main road, Ted managed to hitch a ride to the casualty ward of the local hospital.

There, he was met by a doctor dressed for the operating theatre.

'Don't worry, mate,' said the doctor as he loaded Ted onto the trolley. 'Those slices are very neat. We'll have your fingers back on in no time. Just hand them over.'

'What do you mean, "hand them over"?' quizzed Ted.

'Bloody hell,' sighed the doctor. 'With the miracles of microsurgery, surely, as a carpenter, you knew to save your fingers?'

'Right,' replied Ted indignantly, 'and just how did you expect me to pick them up?'

★★★

Three mental patients attempt to escape from the psychiatric ward. The first patient crawls past the head nurse's desk and meows. Then the second patient crawls past the head nurse's desk and also meows. Midway through crawling past the head nurse's desk, the third mental patient leaps up and bellows, 'Hey, nursie! I'm a cat, just like those other blokes!'

★★★

A couple of hunters are out in the bush when one of them falls to the ground. He doesn't seem to be breathing, and his eyes are rolled back in his head. The other guy whips out his

mobile phone and calls 000. He gasps to the
operator, 'My friend is dead! What can I do?'
The operator, in a calm, soothing voice says,
'Just take it easy. I can help. First, let's be sure
that he's really dead.'
There is silence, then a shot is heard ...
The hunter says, 'Okay, now what?'

***

Old Bluey is suddenly convinced that he is a chicken. He'd start each morning by scratching around in the dirt and making loud 'BRAAARRK-AAAARK!' clucking noises.

A worried mate takes Bluey's missus aside and says, 'What's going on with Bluey thinking that he's a chicken? Can't you take him to a shrink?'

'What?' says Bluey's missus, shocked. 'You expect me to stop getting free eggs?'

★★★

A little girl was playing in the garden when she spotted two spiders mating.

'Daddy, what are those two spiders doing?' she asked.

'They're mating, darling,' her father replied.

'And what do you call the spider on top, Daddy?' she asked.

'That's a daddy-long-legs, sweetheart,' her father answered.

'Does that mean that the other spider is a mummy-long-legs?' said the little girl sweetly.

'No, honey. It's a daddy-long-legs, too.'

'WELL!' huffs the little girl, stamping her foot on top of the two spiders. 'We're not having any of that poofter crap in my garden!'

'Are you concerned about this "Mad Cow Disease"?' said one cow to another.
'No,' replied the other creature, 'and that would be because I'm a duck.'

***

'I am Napoleon!' shrieks one patient at the mental hospital.
'And how do you know that?' asks the psych nurse.
'God told me!'

'Why, I certainly did not!' comes a voice from the next room.

★★★

A man thinks that he's got a bit of a problem – he's started having sex with biscuits. So he goes to the psychiatrist for an assessment. 'Before I can determine whether or not you've got a serious problem, I want to talk about the biscuits. So, these biscuits you're having sex with, are they rich and indulgent chocolate biscuits like Tim Tams?' asks the psychiatrist. 'Nope,' replies the bloke. 'Okay, so are they more your shortbread variety of biscuit, good for dunking in tea?' 'Uh-uh, no sir,' says the man, shaking his head. 'I see – so, are they like those dry biscuits that you serve at parties topped with gherkins and cheese?' 'Yeah! Those are the exact biscuits that I've been having sex with!' exclaims the bloke. 'Well, if that's the case,' replies the quack, 'I can quite safely say that you're f***ing crackers!'

★★★

Johnno was down at the pub with his dog Fido one Saturday evening when the footy results came up on the telly. Johnno's team had won by miles, and Fido started barking and running around chasing his tail.

'That's amazing!' says the barman, 'So what does Fido do when your team loses?'

'He does back-flips,' smiles Johnno.

'Really? How many?' asks the barman.

'That depends on how hard I kick him.'

To the Downright Useless

Insults

You're as useful as a one-legged bloke in an arse-kicking contest.

You couldn't knock the skin off a rice pudding.

You're as useful as an arsehole on a broom.

If your brains were lard, you couldn't grease a frying pan.

You couldn't give away presents in an orphanage at Christmas.

You're as useful as a submarine with flywire doors.

You're as useful as a glass door on a dunny.

★★★

What are ya, blind Freddie?

★★★

Did your parents ever ask you to run away from home?

★★★

You're as useful as an ejector-seat in a helicopter.

★★★

You're as useful as an ashtray on a pushbike.

★★★

You're not worth a pinch of goat shit.

★★★

You're a bloomin' ninny.

★★★

You couldn't give away cheese at a rats' picnic.

★★★

You couldn't give away condoms to a cricket team partying with a bunch of supermodels.

★★★

You're like a pimple on a pumpkin.

★★★

You couldn't make glue out of flour and water.

★★★

You're the kind of bloke that would make a great blueprint for an idiot.

★★★

You couldn't last a round in a revolving door.

★★★

Do you ever have that terrible empty feeling - in your skull?

★★★

You're just a big girl's blouse.

★★★

You're as useful as boobs on a bull.

★★★

You couldn't run a chook raffle in a country pub.

★★★

You're as useful as the bottom half of a mermaid.

★★★

You couldn't organise a root in a brothel.

★★★

You couldn't train a passionfruit vine over a country dunny.

★★★

You're the one that John West rejected.

★★★

You couldn't give away Lindt to a chocoholic.

★★★

You're as useful as a waterproof teabag.

★★★

You couldn't win if you started the night before.

★★★

You must have got your licence out of a Cornflakes packet.

★★★

You're as useful as a pocket on a singlet.

★★★

You've only got one oar in the water.

★★★

You're as useful as a spare prick at a wedding.

★★★

You're as weak as a wet whistle.

★★★

You're as weak as cat's piss.

★★★

You couldn't fart into a bottle.

★★★

You couldn't fight your way out of a paper bag.

★★★

You're as useful as a pogo-stick in quicksand.

★★★

You're as useful as rubber lips on a woodpecker.

★★★

You couldn't direct traffic down a one-way street.

★★★

You couldn't fall off a fence in a gale.

★★★

You couldn't hit the side of a woolshed.

★★★

You couldn't find your shadow at midday.

★★★

You couldn't get a kick in a stampede.

★★★

You couldn't find water if you fell down a well.

★★★

You're not the full stubby.

★★★

Good one, numbnuts!

★★★

You couldn't pull a greasy stick out of a dead dog's arse.

★★★

You couldn't hit a cow in the tit with a tin can.

★★★

You're as useful as a bucket under a bull.

★★★

You're a spastic!

★★★

Get off the grass!

★★★

You're as useful as a third armpit.

★★★

You're as useful as two knobs of billy-goat poop.

★★★

You'd burn down the house trying to make ice-cream.

★★★

You're as useful as a one-armed juggler.

★★★

You couldn't put out a fire in a matchbox if you pissed on it.

★★★

You're as useful as a windscreen wiper on a submarine.

★★★

You're a 24-carat pissant.

You're so useless, if you had a third hand you'd need another pocket to put it in.

You're as useful as a one-legged tightrope walker.

You're as useful as a trap-door on a lifeboat.

You're so useless, if you shouted "Coo-ee!" across King's Canyon, you wouldn't get an echo.

Jokes

A Northern Territory jackaroo radios back to the station.

'Boss, I've got a hell of a problem. I hit a pig with the ute. The pig's okay, but he's stuck in the bull-bars at the front of my ute. He's wriggling and squealing so much that I can't get him out.'

The station manager says, 'Rightio, there's a 303 behind the seat. Take it, shoot the pig in the head and you'll be able to remove him.'

Five minutes later, the jackaroo calls back. 'I did what you said, boss. Took the 303, shot the pig in the head and removed him from the bull-bars. No problem there, but I still can't go on about my business.'

'What's the bloody problem now?' raged the station manager.

'Well, boss, it's his motorbike. You see, the flashing blue light is stuck under the right-front wheelarch.'

An agitated guy rushes into a bar and orders a double Scotch.

'Mate, how tall do you reckon penguins grow?' he blurts to the barman.

'Gee, they're pretty small. I'd say they'd grow to be about two feet, wouldn't they?' says the barman.

'Oh shit!' shrieks the guy, banging his head on the bar in dismay. 'I think I just ran over a nun!'

★★★

After falling from the twentieth storey of a high-rise apartment building in Surfer's Paradise, the blonde lay bruised, shocked and sore on the footpath.

A crowd quickly gathered and moments later a policeman pushed his way past the onlookers.

'What happened?' he asked the blonde.
'Gee, I don't know,' she replied. 'I only just got here myself.'

★★★

Kevin and Bruce were in desperate need of jobs so they bought a newspaper and looked through the employment section. They found an advertisement stating the following: 'Two butlers needed for a Scottish country manner. References a must.'
The job sounded ideal, but the one problem was that they didn't have references. Solution? Easy. Kevin wrote Bruce's reference and Bruce wrote Kevin's reference. They then took a bus to the manor and offered the lady of the manor their references. But she waved them aside, saying, 'We'll get on to that later. First, I'd like to check your knees. Formal wear here means wearing kilts, so if you would be so kind as to drop the tweeds.'
The lads thought this was a little strange, but did as requested.
'Not bad,' she said. 'Now you can show me your testimonials.'
When they picked themselves up from the gravel driveway, Kevin sighed, 'With a little more education, we would have got that job, Bruce.'

★★★

A bloke comes home early from work and hears strange noises coming from the bedroom. He rushes upstairs to find his wife naked on the bed, sweating and panting. 'What's wrong?' he asks.

'I'm having a heart attack!' she cries.

The bloke rushes downstairs to grab the telephone, but just as he's dialling, his youngest boy comes up to him and says, 'Daddy! Daddy! Uncle Ted's hiding in your wardrobe and he hasn't got any clothes on!'

The bloke slams down the phone and storms upstairs into the bedroom, past his screaming wife, and rips open the wardrobe door. Sure enough, there's his brother Ted, totally naked, cowering on the floor.

'You rotten mongrel,' says the husband. 'My wife's having a heart attack, and you're running around naked scaring the kids!'

★★★

In the schoolyard, one kid says to another: 'You know, one in five people in the world are of Chinese origin. My family has five people, so, according to this statistic, one of us must be Chinese. It's either me, my mum, my dad, or my older sister Tiffany. I guess there's a slight possibility that it's my younger sister Mun-ha Lee. But I really think it must be Tiffany.'

★★★

A buxom beauty visits the G.P. with a very young baby.

She says, 'Doctor, the baby just isn't feeding. I'm worried that he's becoming malnourished.'

After examining the infant, the doctor decides that he is a little underweight.

'Tell me, ma'am, is the child breastfed?'

'Yes, he is,' comes the reply.

'Well, if you'll remove your blouse, I'd best examine you to see if everything's okay.'

The woman sits up on the examining table, and the doctor carefully weighs each ample breast in his hands. Perplexed and a little flustered, the doctor says, 'If you don't mind ma'am, I'm going to attach a breast-pump.'

The beauty willingly complies.

After a few minutes of switching the pump on various settings, the doctor exclaims, 'Well, I can see that there definitely is a problem – you have no milk!'

The beauty laughs, 'Oh, there's no problem there, doctor! I'm just the babysitter.'

★★★

A girl from the wrong side of the tracks goes to Social Security to register for childcare benefits.

'How many children do you have?' asked the human services officer.

'Twelve,' answered the girl.

'Twelve?' replied the officer incredulously. 'What are their names?'

'Well, there's Billy, Billy, Billy, Billy, Billy, Billy, Billy, Billy, Billy, Billy, Billy and Billy,' recites the girl.

'Doesn't that get confusing with them all having the same name?'

'Nah,' said the girl. 'It's great because if they are out playing in the street, I just have to shout, "BILLY, YOUR DINNER'S READY!" or "BILLY, DO YOUR HOMEWORK!" and they all do as they're told.'

'And what if you only want to speak to one of the boys individually?' quizzes the officer.

'Easy,' said the girl. 'I just use their surnames.'

★★★

A bloke was given a council job painting the white lines down the centre of a highway. On his first day he painted for twelve kilometres; on his second day he painted for six kilometres, and on his third day he painted for less than a kilometre.

'Listen here, mate,' said the foreman. 'On your first day you were going great guns, but how come you're doing less and less painting each day?'

'Well, you've got to cut me some slack!' snapped the bloke defensively. 'Each day I get further and further away from the can of paint!'

***

A skydiver leaps from a plane only to discover that his parachute has failed. Plummeting towards the Earth, he is shocked to notice another man on his way up.
'Oi, mate!' he cries across the great blue yonder, 'Do you know anything about parachutes?'
'Sorry, buddy,' says the other bloke sadly shaking his head. 'Do you know anything about gas ovens?'

BOOM!

***

An Italian boy and a Jewish boy come of age
at the same time. The Italian boy's father
presents him with a brand new pistol. On the
other side of town, at his Bar Mitzvah, the
Jewish boy receives a beautiful gold watch.
The next day when the two boys see each
other at school they show each other what
they got. It turns out that each boy likes the
other's present better, and so they trade. That
night, when the Italian boy is at home, his
father sees him looking at the watch.
'Where you getta thatta watch?' asks the father.
The boy explains that he and his Jewish friend
had traded. The father blows his top.
'Whatta you? Stupidda boy? Whatsa matta you?
Somma day, you maybe gonna getta married.
Then maybe somma day you gonna comma
home and finda you wife inna bed with
another man. Whatta you gonna do then?
Looka atta you watch and say, "How longa
you gonna be?"'

To the Hideously Ugly

Insults

You could eat an apple through a picket fence.

★★★

Your head stands out like a black crow in a bucket of milk.

★★★

A brickie's arse has a nicer smile than yours.

★★★

I've seen better heads on a glass of beer.

★★★

You've got teeth like a row of condemned houses.

★★★

You've got more arse than class.

★★★

When you enter a room, the mice jump on chairs.

★★★

I've seen better heads on a bumful of boils.

★★★

You've got a head like a Mini with the doors open.

★★★

You could open a can of sliced pineapple with that nose.

★★★

When you're out bushwalking, bunyip sightings go up one hundred per cent.

★★★

You're all behind in Melbourne.

★★★

Do you need a licence to be that ugly?

★★★

You're so ugly, your mum hides the baby photos.

★★★

I've seen better heads on a backful of acne.

★★★

You could eat the arse out of a low-flying duck with those chompers.

★★★

You've got hair like a dunny brush and shitty breath to match.

★★★

You're as bald as a bandicoot.

★★★

You're so ugly, even your shadow walks on the other side of the street.

★★★

When you were born, your mum asked that they put you back.

★★★

You belong to the hairy-legs and floppy-tits brigade.

★★★

You don't need plastic surgery – the wrecker's will do.

★★★

You've got hair like a bush-pig's arse.

★★★

I've peeled better-looking faces off my roo-bar.

★★★

You're uglier than the north-facing end of a south-bound camel.

You're as skinny as a sapling with the bark scraped off.

★★★

If my dog had a face like yours, I'd shave his arse and make him walk backwards.

★★★

You've got a verandah above the toy shop.

★★★

When you were born, the doctor slapped your mother.

★★★

If you went to the dermatologist, he'd prescribe a paper bag.

★★★

You've got a mug that's perfect for radio.

★★★

Your schnoz sticks out like a dog's balls.

★★★

If you went to the plastic surgeon, he'd ask if you wanted a tail.

You're broad in the beam.

★★★

When you were little, the bogey-man worried that you were hiding under his bed.

★★★

Not even the tide would take you out.

★★★

So you were born on a farm – were there any more in the litter?

★★★

If you went to the beautician, they'd spend twelve hours on the quote.

★★★

Your head is like a robber's dog.

★★★

Your thighs wouldn't stop a pig in a hall.

★★★

I've seen prettier faces on a pirate flag.

★★★

It's a bloke's right to be ugly, but you're taking advantage.

★★★

You couldn't cop a root in a brothel.

★★★

When you cry, the tears run up your face.

★★★

What time are you leaving, bargearse?

★★★

I've seen better legs in a chook shed.

★★★

It's faces like yours that remind people to use birth-control.

★★★

So, you grew up in the circus?

★★★

Your missus goes to work with you just so she doesn't have to kiss you goodbye.

★★★

You're so ugly, you make onions cry.

★★★

When you go to the dentist, he prefers that you keep your mouth closed.

★★★

You're so ugly, the dog takes himself for a walk.

★★★

You're all done up like a pox-doctor's clerk.

★★★

You're as pretty as a box of blowflies.

★★★

If you walked past the butcher's, he'd throw you a bone.

★★★

If you stay still too long, the cat covers you in kitty-litter.

★★★

You ought to wear a sign around your neck that reads: "This way up!"

★★★

You're as pretty as a hatful of arseholes.

★★★

You're so ugly, the kids feed you dog biscuits.

Jokes

Tony comes back from a tour of Thailand. While he was there, he visited a few of the brothels in Bangkok's red-light district, and came home with an unsightly skin disease. 'Your skin disease is a real problem, Tony,' chided the doctor. 'We're going to have to put you on a strict diet of pizzas and pancakes.' 'Pizzas and pancakes?' gasped Tony. 'How are they going to help clear my skin?' 'Well, I don't know about your skin,' laughs the doctor. 'But those foods will shove nicely under your door because you'll probably be eating alone nowadays.'

A bloke comes home from a long night on the tiles. 'Sweetheart,' he slurs to his wife, 'my mate Johnno reckons he's had sex with every woman on this street except one. What do you reckon about that?' 'Hmmph!' snorts his missus, 'I bet it's that ugly cow Mrs Brown next door.'

A rather tired-looking woman in her fifties visits a cosmetic surgeon asking if he can make her look youthful again.

'I certainly can, madam!' he says obligingly. 'Now, all it's going to take is for me to remove those bags under your eyes with a little nip and tuck, and I can tighten the skin to eliminate your crow's feet. Once I'm done, you'll look 40 again.'

'Forty!' the woman splutters, 'I want to look 22. How can you achieve that?'

'Well,' the doctor replies uncertainly as he looks her over, 'I guess I could give you botox injections on your forehead to remove those frown lines. I could add some cheek implants to even out those jowls. For your double chin, I'll pull that tight. However, as this area tends to sag, I'll put a little screw in at the base of your skull, and we can tighten it whenever your chin begins to droop.'

So the woman books in for the works and is very happy with the results.

Six months later she's back in the surgery again. 'Doctor! I have these terrible bags under my eyes, please help me!'

'Madam, those are your breasts! And if you don't stop tightening that screw, you'll soon find yourself with a goatee!'

Doris goes into the local cop shop to report that her husband Norm has gone missing. 'Constable, Norm is 26 years old, six foot two inches, has a gorgeous shock of mahogany brown hair, and the body of a prime athlete.'
'Come on, Doris! Who are you trying to kid?' laughs the constable. 'Norm is closer to sixty, he's about five foot, completely bald and grossly overweight.'
'That's right,' sighs Doris, 'but who wants that old bastard back?'

A woman who was trying to interest her husband in a bit of 'action' went to the lounge room where he was watching TV and said, 'Honey, today I went to the doctor for my annual check-up. He had me take off all my clothes and then told me that I have the most beautiful breasts and legs that he'd ever seen.'
'Oh yeah?' sneered her husband. 'What did he say about your fat arse?'
'To be honest, darling,' she replied sweetly, 'your name was never mentioned.'

Husband: 'Drinking makes you look absolutely gorgeous, darling.'
Wife: 'What are you talking about? I haven't had a drop!'
Husband: 'No, but I have.'

★★★

After passionately making love to a beautiful woman that he met in a nightclub a few hours earlier, young Brian is desperately craving a cigarette. He asks the woman if she smokes. She replies that she does, and directs him toward the top drawer of her dressing table. Upon opening the drawer, Brian finds a packet of smokes and a framed photograph of a burly bikie covered in tattoos.
'Er ... who's the bloke in the photo?' he asks, a little nervously. 'He isn't your boyfriend, is he?'
'Oh no!' titters the girl, 'That's me before the operation.'

★★★

A woman with a pram steps on a bus headed to Circular Quay.
'Dear Lord!' shrieks the bus driver, 'That would have to be the UGLIEST kid I've ever seen.'
Furious, the woman slams down her fare and advises the bus driver to keep his opinions to himself. In a flood of tears, she bustles her way to the back of the bus.

A few stops later, a man gets on the bus with a bunch of flowers and sits next to the woman and her pram. He notices that she's been crying and passes her a long-stemmed rose. He smiles gently, 'Here, ma'am. This might help brighten your day.'

The woman wipes her tears, accepts the flower, quietly sobs that she's very grateful for his kindness.

'Oh, it doesn't stop there!' smiles the man, reaching into his pocket and removing a banana, 'This is a little treat for your monkey.'

Why did God invent alcohol?
So ugly people could have sex.

Barry was overweight. He had tried every crash diet around, but just couldn't seem to move the kilos, and was starting to lose hope. One day, as he was tucking into a huge portion of fish and chips, Barry noticed an advertisement on the wrapper for yet another diet clinic. It read: 'Sex Diet: Lose Kilos the Fun Way!'

Without a moment's hesitation, Barry shoved another potato cake in his mouth and called the 'Sex Diet' hotline. The woman who answered advised that it cost $20 for each ten kilograms of weight he lost. Barry had about thirty kilograms to lose, and decided to go for it, relaying his credit card details over the line. 'Right, tonight just after dinner, one of our luscious ladies will knock on your door,' the hotline operator promised. 'Make sure you're right and ready to go.'

Sure enough, as soon as he'd tucked away his last piece of fried chicken for the evening, there came a knock at the door. On his doorstep was a stunning redhead in a PVC tracksuit.

'Okay, honey,' she snapped. 'You catch me, you can screw me.' And with that she bolted down the street. Barry huffed and puffed for a good hour or so, running around the suburb. He didn't catch her, but did come pretty close. However, by the time he got home, the extreme energy expended whilst chasing this bodacious babe had depleted an amazing ten kilograms from his frame.

The next week, Barry made another phone call to the 'Sex Diet' hotline. 'Right, I lost ten kilos last time, and now I'd like to lose another ten!' he said.

'Sure. But the price has gone up. The second ten kilos costs $200,' came the reply.

'Aaah, why not,' smiled Barry, knowing that every dollar was worth it. He was certain that he'd catch the girl now that he was ten kilos lighter. He came pretty close last time.

Sure enough, once he'd finished off his second pizza for the night, there came a knock at the door. On his doorstep was a ravishing blonde in a PVC tracksuit.

'Here goes, sweetheart,' she smirked. 'You catch me, you screw me.' And with that, she bolted down the street. Barry huffed and puffed for a good hour or so, running around the suburb, but he didn't catch her. However, by the time he got home, the extreme energy expended whilst chasing this foxy filly had depleted another ten kilograms from his frame.

The next week, Barry made another phone call to the 'Sex Diet' hotline. 'Right, I lost ten kilos the last two times, and now I'd like to lose yet another ten!' he said.

'Sure, but the third ten kilos is going to cost you $2000,' came the reply.

'That's cool,' chuckled Barry, knowing that he was fitter and faster than ever before. This time he'd definitely catch whatever vixen they threw his way.

Sure enough, once he'd finished off his tray of nachos for the night, there came a knock at the door. But this time, it was the fattest, ugliest, smelliest and most entirely repulsive woman he'd ever seen.

'Okey-doke,' she leered, 'I paid good money

for this. They say that if I can catch you, I can screw you ...'

★★★

A guy walks into a chemist and asks for a bottle of Viagra. The chemist eyes him suspiciously and asks, 'Do you have a prescription for that?'
'No,' says the guy shaking his head, 'but will this photo of my wife do?'

★★★

Young King Arthur was ambushed and imprisoned by the monarch of a neighbouring kingdom. The monarch could have killed him, but was moved by Arthur's youth and ideals. So the monarch offered him freedom, as long as he could answer a very difficult question. Arthur would have a year to figure out the answer; if, after a year, he still had no answer, he would be put to death. The question: What do women really want?
Such a question would perplex even the most knowledgeable man, and, to young Arthur, it seemed an impossible query. But, since it was better than death, he accepted the monarch's proposition to have an answer by year's end.
He returned to his kingdom and began to poll everybody: the princesses, the prostitutes, the cooks, the priests, the wise men, the serving

wenches, the court jester. He spoke with everyone, but no one could give him a satisfactory answer. Many people advised him to consult the old witch – only she would know the answer. The price would be high; the witch was famous throughout the kingdom for the exorbitant prices she charged.

The last day of the year arrived, and Arthur had no alternative but to talk to the witch. She agreed to answer his question, but he'd have to accept her price first: the old witch wanted to marry Sir Gawain, the most noble of the Knights of the Round Table and Arthur's closest friend! Young Arthur was horrified: she was hunchbacked and hideous, had only one tooth, smelled like sewage, made obscene noises, etc. He had never encountered such a repugnant creature. He refused to force his friend to marry her, and have to endure such a burden.

Sir Gawain, upon learning of the proposal, spoke with Arthur. He told him that nothing was too big a sacrifice compared to Arthur's life and the preservation of the Round Table. Hence, their wedding was proclaimed, and the witch answered Arthur's question thus: what a woman really wants is to be in charge of her own life. Everyone instantly knew that the witch had uttered a great truth and that Arthur's life would be spared. And so it was.

The neighbouring monarch granted Arthur total freedom.

What a wedding Sir Gawain and the witch had! Arthur was torn between relief and anguish. Gawain was proper as always, gentle and courteous. The old witch put her worst manners on display, and generally made everyone very uncomfortable.

The honeymoon hour approached. Sir Gawain, steeling himself for a horrific experience, entered the bedroom. But what a sight awaited him! The most beautiful woman he'd ever seen lay before him! The astounded Sir Gawain asked what had happened. The beauty replied that since he had been so kind to her when she'd appeared as a witch, she would henceforth be her horrible, deformed self half the time, and the other half, she would be her beautiful maiden self. Which would he want her to be during the day, and which during the night?

What a cruel question! Sir Gawain pondered his predicament. During the day, he could have a beautiful woman to show off to his friends, but at night, in the privacy of his home, he'd share his bed with an old witch? Or would he prefer having by day a hideous witch, but by night a beautiful woman with whom to enjoy many intimate moments? The noble Sir Gawain replied that he would let her choose for herself.

Upon hearing this, she announced that she would be beautiful all the time, because he had respected her enough to let her be in charge of her own life.

And what is the moral of this story?

If your woman doesn't get her own way, things are going to get ugly!

To the Plain Drunk

Insults

You're away with the pixies.

★★★

You're blind.

★★★

You're belly-dancing with the hippos.

★★★

You're as full as a fairy's phone book.

★★★

You're as full as a fat woman's sock.

★★★

You're as full as a goog.

★★★

You're stonkered.

★★★

You're stunned.

★★★

You're tanked.

★★★

You're blotto.

★★★

You're tired and emotional.

★★★

You're zonked.

★★★

You're under the affluence of incohol.

★★★

You're three parts gone.

★★★

You're as drunk as a skunk.

★★★

If you needed a blood transfusion, the ambos would fill you up at CUB.

★★★

You're smashed.

★★★

You're wearing the wobbly gumboot.

★★★

You're as full as a state school.

★★★

You're as full as a tick.

★★★

You're legless.

★★★

You're bloomin' Molly the monk.

★★★

You're as full as a fat woman's undies.

★★★

You're as full as a tuckshop at recess.

★★★

You're lit up like a Christmas tree.

★★★

You're dead to the world.

★★★

You're as pissed as a possum.

★★★

You're away with the birdies.

★★★

You're as loaded as a truckie's dinner-plate.

★★★

You're as pissed as a parrot.

★★★

You're as full as a boot.

★★★

You're as drunk as Chloe.

★★★

You're out to it.

★★★

You're paralytic.

★★★

You're as pissed as a newt.

★★★

You're as rotten as a chop.

★★★

You're so loaded, QANTAS makes you travel in cargo.

★★★

You're shot full of holes.

★★★

You've got a mouth like a camel-driver's crotch.

★★★

You're a two-pot screamer.

★★★

Your idea of exercise is hiccupping on the bar-stool.

★★★

You're two-and-a-half sheets to the wind.

★★★

You're as pissed as a kiddie's mattress.

★★★

You're shickered.

★★★

You're shellacked.

★★★

You're shit-faced.

★★★

You're a pisspot.

★★★

Your job interferes with your drinking.

★★★

Your mouth's like the bottom of a cocky's cage.

★★★

You'd call your kids Barley and Hops.

★★★

You're as pissed as a fart in a vacuum.

★★★

You're lit up like a Manly ferry.

★★★

You're a bag-over-the-head job.

★★★

The doctor would be lucky to find blood in your alcohol-stream.

★★★

You'd try drinking a nip in the air.

★★★

If I gave you a light, you'd burn for days.

★★★

Your idea of a balanced diet is a tinnie in each hand.

★★★

You're as pissed as a fart.

★★★

You're such a pisshead, you'd write 'Johnnie Walker' as next of kin.

★★★

Jokes

Feeling a little bit toey, a drunk decided to visit a prostitute. Unfortunately, he was so inebriated that he mistakenly walked into a podiatrist's office. Winking lewdly at the receptionist, he said, 'Hey love, ya know what I'm here for!'

She said she did know what he was there for, and told him to go into the doctor's office, sit on the examining table, and place his extremity on the cushion.

The drunk did as he was told, unzipping his fly and putting his privates on the cushion. When the nurse came back in, she yelled, 'Hey, that's not a foot!'

Perplexed, the drunk replied, 'Since when is there a minimum?'

What's the difference between a drunk and an alcoholic?
A drunk doesn't have to bother attending all those boring meetings.

After closing time, two drunks staggered past a bus depot.

'Hey, let's steal a bus so we can drive home,' slurred one drunk.

The other drunk peered bleary-eyed through the mesh fence, 'Don't bother,' he mumbled to his mate. 'The number 253 to East Brunswick is right down the back. We'll never get it out.'

★★★

After going to the toilet late one night, old Johnno came back to bed and proclaimed to his missus that he'd just witnessed a miracle.

'You see, when I went into the bathroom the light went on all by itself. Then when I'd finished my business, the light went off all by itself,' gasped Johnno.

'That's no miracle,' scoffed his missus, 'you're bloody drunk and you've pissed in the fridge again!'

★★★

Bob and Dave are in a bar, sharing a few beers.

'You know what, Dave? I didn't have sex with my wife until we were married. How about you?' says Bob.

'I dunno,' replies Dave. 'What was her maiden name?'

The drunk said to his friend on a street corner one night, 'You know, mate, I'll never ever forget the first time I turned to the bottle as a substitute for women.'

'How come?' asked his friend, 'What happened?'

The drunk replied, 'I got my penis stuck and needed a cork remover.'

***

Bruce was at the pub one night, downing a few, when he noticed the guy next to him slide off his seat and land on the floor. Being good at heart, Bruce decides to help the guy home. He manages to get the guy's address from the bartender, puts his arm around the guy's waist and struggles to get him out the door.

No sooner do they hit the street, when the man's legs crumple beneath him and he falls into a gutter. Bruce helps him up, and once again the man falls over.

Bruce is getting a bit annoyed now and says to the semi-conscious man, 'Jesus, mate, surely at your age you should know when to stop drinking!'

After a couple more attempts at getting the guy to stand up, Bruce gives up and throws the guy over his shoulder.

When he reaches the man's house, Bruce knocks grumpily on the door and says to the woman who answers, 'Here's your husband. If I were you I'd have a bit of a chat with him about his drinking problem.'

'I will,' she promises. 'But tell me, where's his wheelchair?'

A young athlete was doing push-ups in the park when a drunk staggered past, and then came back and laughed at him.

'What's so funny,' said the athlete indignantly.

'I hate to tell you this,' slurred the drunk, 'but your girlfriend's gone home!'

★★★

A bloke with a few beers under his belt stumbles up his driveway to find his son working on the family car.

'What's bloody wrong this time?' he slurs.

'Piston broke,' replies his son.

'Yeah? Well, so am I.'

★★★

A drunk stumbles upon a baptism service one Sunday afternoon down by the river. The minister turns to him and says, 'Mister, are you ready to find Jesus?'

The drunk looks around him and slurs, 'Yes, sir, I am!'

The minister then dunks the fellow under the water and pulls him right back up.

'Have you found Jesus?' the minister asks.

'No, I have not!' gasps the drunk.

The minister dunks him again, brings him up and says, 'Now, brother, have you found Jesus?'

'No, I have not!' gasps the drunk again.

Rolling his eyes, the minister holds the man under the water for quite a long time, brings him up and demands, 'For the love of God, have you found Jesus yet?'

The old drunk wipes his eyes and pleads, 'Are you sure this is where he fell in?'

★★★

To the Mean and Stingy

Insults

You're so stingy, you wouldn't give a rat a railway pie.

***

You're as mean as a bookie on Cup Day.

***

You'd give 20 cents to a plastic guide dog and crack it open for change.

***

You're as mean as bird shit.

***

On a Sunday drive, you'd make the missus push to save petrol.

***

You're so tight, you'd bring Tupperware to a wake.

***

If I wanted to hear from an arsehole, I'd fart.

***

When you have a party, your guests bring their own scotch ... and their own rocks.

***

You wouldn't give away the steam off your shit.

★★★

If a fly walked over your butter, you'd lick the fly.

★★★

You wouldn't shout in a shark attack.

★★★

May all your chooks turn into emus and kick your dunny door down!

★★★

You're so mean, your kids get one measle at a time.

★★★

You're tighter than Warwick Capper's footy shorts.

★★★

You're as cunning as a shithouse rat.

★★★

You're so tight, you've got a Rottweiler guarding your rubbish bin.

You're tighter than a cow's arse in blowfly season.

★★★

You're mingy.

★★★

You're so cheap, you'd tell your kids that Santa died in a plane crash on Christmas Eve.

★★★

You're meaner than a stepmother's kiss.

★★★

When you take a dollar out of your pocket, Queen Elizabeth blinks at the light.

★★★

You're so tight, when someone rings your doorbell, the kids have to yell, "Ding dong!"

★★★

You're meaner than an insurance company after a flood.

★★★

You're so cheap, you went on your honeymoon alone.

★★★

You're so tight, you could stick a chunk of coal up your arse and it would come out a diamond.

***

Jokes

Two couples were enjoying a game of poker when John accidentally drops a card on the floor. When he bends down under the table to pick it up, he notices that Greg's wife Carol isn't wearing any underwear. Shocked, he hits his head on the table and emerges slightly flushed.

Later, when John goes to get himself a beer, Carol follows him into the kitchen and asks, 'So, did you see anything under the table that you liked, John?'

John admits that he did.

Carol replies, 'Well, it's all yours for just $100. Greg's working late on Friday night, so how about coming over at eight?'

On Friday night, John turns up at eight o'clock sharp, pays Carol $100 and they go on to enjoy an hour of lovemaking.

Around midnight, Greg comes home. He asks his wife, 'So, John came by tonight, did he?'

Carol flushes a deep beetroot and splutters, 'Er ... yes.'

'And he gave you a hundred bucks?' said John.

'Um ... yes, he did. How did you know?'

'Well, he came by the office this morning and borrowed the money. He said that he'd stop by and see you tonight. I was just worried that the shifty bastard wouldn't pay me back!'

★★★

How is the census taken in Israel?

They roll a coin down the street.

★★★

Mr Webb, head of a local charity, was irritated because Mr Somers, one of the wealthiest men in town, still had not given his charity a donation. Mr Webb rang Mr Somers in order to give it his last shot. 'Sir, it is known throughout this town that you're exceedingly wealthy. Would you be so kind as to share your good fortune with our organisation so that we can continue helping those in need?'

Mr Somers replied, 'Listen, is it also known throughout this town that I have a widowed, dying mother who has no source of income? Or a sister whose husband was killed and she now has eight hungry mouths to support alone? Or a brother who lost both arms and legs in a bad car accident?'

After some pause he added, 'And ... if I don't

give my money to them, why the hell should I give it to you?'

★★★

Bluey was stone-cold broke. His wife had left him, he had alimony to pay for his five kids, and his business had gone completely arse-up. He turned to religion, 'Almighty Lord,' he prayed, 'please allow me to win the lottery, I promise to use my money for good and I'll come to church every Sunday.'

Bluey was disappointed when he didn't win the lottery, so prayed again, 'Almighty Lord, perhaps you didn't hear me last time, but if you allow me to win the lottery, I promise to use my money for good and I'll come to church every Saturday *and* Sunday.'

Once again, Bluey was disappointed when he didn't win the lottery, so had another go at praying, 'Almighty Lord! I've prayed to you twice now. If you let me win the lottery, I promise to use my money for good and I'll come to church every Saturday, Sunday and Wednesday!'

'Bluey, Bluey, Bluey!' boomed a voice from the heavens. 'I've heard you praying all these times, and I'm more than pleased to meet you halfway. But first, you must buy a lottery ticket.'

Two business men, working away from home a lot, decided to share a mistress. They set her up in her own apartment, sharing the expenses equally between them. One day the mistress told the two men she was pregnant. Wanting to do the right thing, the men agreed to split the costs of bringing up the child. When the mistress went into hospital, only one of the businessmen was in town to be there for the birth of the baby. When the other one returned, he went to the hospital to visit the newborn. His friend was sitting on the hospital steps looking depressed. 'What's wrong? Were there problems with the birth?' 'Oh, she's fine, but I have some bad news. She had twins, and mine died.'

★★★

After the family home burned down, Mrs Smith rang AAMI.
'Listen here, our house has burned down and it was worth $250,000. I want my money right away!'
'Excuse me, ma'am,' replied the operator, 'I'm afraid that insurance doesn't work quite like that. A representative from the insurance company needs to assess the value of what was insured and we will then provide you

with replacement items of the same worth.'
'Right,' says Mrs Smith, 'in that case, I'd like to cancel my husband's life insurance.'

★★★

After torrential downpours and floods cutting off all surrounding roads, a family on a sheep station finds their home isolated for several weeks. Eventually, the Red Cross are able to send a rescue mission out to the station and they come knocking upon the door.
'Who is it?' barks a suspicious voice from inside.
'It's the Red Cross, we're here to –'
'We donated last year,' interrupts the station manager. 'And with these floods drowning all our sheep, we're flamin' broke, so bugger off!'

★★★

A couple had been spending far too much money, so decided that they'd adopt a brand new savings plan. The husband said that every time they had sex, he'd put $20 into a piggybank.
Around a year later, the husband decides to empty the piggybank.
'I've been putting $20 notes in this piggybank each time we have sex, yet there are $50 notes and $100 notes in here also!' he shrieks.

'What's been going on?'

'That's half your trouble,' sniffs his wife, 'not everyone is quite as cheap as you!'

***

Eira and Josef were walking down the street when they spotted a sign outside St Patrick's Cathedral that read: Anyone who converts to Catholicism will get a $500 bonus.'

Eira looked wistfully at the sign and said, 'Wow – $500 – that's such a lot of money.'

Josef looked at him in surprise, 'Eira, surely you wouldn't betray your Jewish heritage for a mere $500!'

'I don't know,' said Eira. 'It's a lot of money. Wait here for me; I'll be right back.'

And with that he entered the cathedral. A short while later he came out and Josef said to

him, 'So, Eira, did you get your $500?'
Eira turned to him with an exasperated look
and said, 'You know, Josef, that's the problem
with you Jews. Everything always comes
down to money, money, money.'

***

A man was reading the paper when he saw an advertisement saying: 'Porsche for sale! Brand new – only $100.'

The guy thought there must have been a misprint, but he thought, 'Well, why not, what have I got to lose?'

So he went to the address and met the lady who was selling the car.

After talking to her for a while he learnt that yes, the Porsche was brand new, and it really was only $100.

'I'll take it!' he said. 'But why are you selling me this great Porsche for only $100?'

The lady replied with a bitter laugh, 'My husband just ran off with his secretary, and he told me, "You can have the house and the furniture, but sell my Porsche and send me the money."'

When the office printer's type began to grow faint, the office manager called a local repair shop where a friendly man informed him that the printer probably needed to be cleaned. Because the store charged $50 for such cleaning, he advised that the manager might try reading the printer's manual and do the job himself.

Pleasantly surprised by his honesty, the office

manager asked, 'Does your boss know that you discourage business?'

'Actually, it's my boss's idea,' the employee replied. 'We usually make more money on repairs if we let people try to fix things themselves first.'

To the Horny Mongrels

Insults

You're as randy as a Mallee bull.

***

You're as frisky as a roo at dusk.

***

You're a root rat.

★★★

You've sown enough wild oats for us to call you Uncle Toby.

★★★

You're in like Flynn.

★★★

You're so randy, you'd root a blind man's dog.

★★★

If you were any hornier, you'd grow a pointy tail and carry a pitchfork.

★★★

You've had more ins and outs than a showground turnstile.

★★★

Newlywed rabbits would have trouble keeping up with you.

★★★

You're the village bike.

★★★

You've had more knickers flung at you than Tom Jones.

★★★

There were so many notches on your bedpost that it turned to sawdust.

★★★

You bang like a dunny door in a gale.

★★★

You're a wombat (eats roots and leaves).

★★★

You're as randy as a bottle of brandy with the 'b' scrubbed out.

★★★

You're a Mallee root.

★★★

You've seen more ceilings than Michelangelo.

★★★

You've seen more Jocks than the Glasgow birth registry.

★★★

You've had more rides than a Greyhound bus.

★★★

You'll be buried in a Y-shaped coffin.

★★★

You've had more scores than a dart board.

★★★

Jokes

With his wife safely out of town on a business trip, old Randy decides to bring his secretary, Betty home. After wining, dining and a bit of slow-dancing, Randy finally manages to get Betty into bed. However, in the throes of passion, he suddenly realises that as a married man he doesn't have any condoms.
Unfortunately, Betty doesn't either.
'Oh, I know!' he says, 'You can use my wife's diaphragm.'
So, after searching the medicine cabinet to no avail, he comes back in a huge huff.
'Sorry, Betty,' he says, switching on the light and killing the mood. 'The fun's over. I knew my missus didn't trust me – the bloomin' cow has taken her diaphragm with her.'

An old codger is explaining to his mate the joys of Viagra.
'I tell you, mate, it's a miracle drug! After just one pill it makes you feel like a man of thirty again.'

'Really?' exclaims the second codger, 'And can you get it over the counter?'

'If you took two,' smiles the first codger, 'I reckon you could.'

★★★

The tomcat, on the prowl as usual, spotted a gorgeous kitten over the fence. He decided to visit her, so gave an almighty leap and landed in her garden. The gorgeous kitten was impressed with the tomcat's big leap, and sauntered over.

'Wow,' she cooed. 'That was amazing. Do you want to go somewhere and get intimate?'

'Erm, afraid not,' said the tomcat, looking pained. 'The fence was higher than I thought.'

★★★

After having thirteen children, Rosa and Luigi decided that they didn't want any more. They went to the doctor to get some advice about birth control. The doctor gave them a box of condoms, and said that if they used them during sex, they wouldn't have any more children. Rosa and Luigi thanked the doctor, then went home.

Two months later they were back in the doctor's office.

'Well,' said the doctor. 'I don't know how you managed it, but Rosa is pregnant again. I

really don't understand how this happened –
did you use the condoms like I told you?'
'Yessa, doctor,' said Rosa. 'We followed alla de
instructions – except that since we no have de
organ, I put it on de tambourine.'

★★★

A captain in the Foreign Legion was
transferred to a desert outpost in central
Australia. On his tour of the area, he noticed a
very old, sickly camel tied up in the back of
the enlisted men's barracks. He asked the
sergeant leading the tour the purpose of the
camel.

The sergeant replied, 'Well, sir, it's a long way
from anywhere, and the men have natural
sexual urges, so when they do, uh, have the
need, we have the camel.'

The captain said, 'Well, if it's good for morale,
then I guess it's all right with me.'

After he had been at the fort for about six
months, the captain couldn't stand his starved-
for-sex life any longer and said to the
sergeant, 'Um, would you mind bringing me
the camel?'

The sergeant shrugged his shoulders and led
the camel into the captain's quarters. The
captain then proceeded to go for it.

Afterwards, he said to the sergeant, 'You know, those guys are onto a good thing with this camel!'

The sergeant replied, 'Well, sir, you're right there, but they usually just use the camel to ride into town.'

***

Old Bertha is widowed and sick of being alone. She puts an ad in a newspaper saying: 'Woman seeking a man who is good in bed, won't abuse her, and won't run away.' Months pass and one day her doorbell rings. She opens the door, and a man with no legs and no arms is in a wheelchair on her porch. Bertha asks, 'Can I help you?'

The man says, 'My name is Lewis and I'm responding to your advert. I've got to tell you, love, I am without a doubt your perfect man.' Narrowing her eyes suspiciously, Bertha replies, 'Oh yeah? And what makes you think that?'

Lewis smiles, 'Well, ma'am, I have no arms so I can't abuse you, and I have no legs so I can't run away.'

Rolling her eyes, Bertha snickers, 'Right, but how do I know that you are good in bed?'

Lewis smirks, 'Well, how do you think I rang the doorbell?'

★★★

One morning, a woman went to a pet shop and immediately spotted a beautiful parrot in a cage near the door. There was a sign on the cage that said $20.

'Why so cheap?' she asked the pet shop owner.

The owner replied, 'Look, I should tell you

first that this bird used to live in a brothel, and sometimes it says some pretty vulgar stuff. That's why I've had to mark her price down.'

The woman thought about this, but decided she had to have the bird anyway. She took it home and hung the bird's cage up in her living room and waited for it to say something. The bird looked around the room, then at her, and said, 'New house, new madam.'

The woman was a bit shocked at the implication, but then thought, 'Oh well, I guess that doesn't really matter.'

When her two teenage daughters returned from school, the bird saw them and said, 'New house, new madam, new whores.'

The girls thought it was a scream. The mother was offended once more, but brushed it off and began laughing with her daughters.

Moments later, the woman's husband, Eric, came home from work.

The bird looked at him and said, 'Oh, hi, Eric.'

★★★

Amber had a problem and eventually decided to see a psychiatrist about it.

'You have to do something to help me!' she wailed to Dr Feelgood. 'Every time I go on a date, I always end up doing all kinds of weird, perverted sexual acts. And then I spend the next day feeling guilty as hell about it.'

'I understand, dear,' said Dr Feelgood. 'We'll have a few sessions together so that we can work on your willpower.'

'No!' Amber responded vehemently. 'I want you to work on getting rid of the guilt.'

★★★

A psychic convention was held in the Brisbane Town Hall one night.

The MC says to the audience, 'Ladies and gentlemen, so that we can realise the common bond we have with each other, I ask for a show of hands – would anyone who has ever heard a voice from the other side please raise their hand.'

At that, 200 hands go up.

'Now, would anybody who has seen a spirit from the other side please raise their hand.' At this about 100 hands go up.

'Would anyone who has ever spoken with, or had any kind of two-way communication with a spirit from the other side – for instance, a ghost – please raise their hand.'

This time only ten hands are raised.

The MC then asked, 'Now, tell me, have any of you ever had any kind of sexual experience with a ghost?'

After a minute of silence, a hand timidly rises at the very back of the room. The hand belongs to Marty, a farmhand.

'You, sir, would you please come up on the stage?' said the MC.

Very shyly, Marty slowly walked from the back of the room up onto the stage.

The MC then said, 'Sir, this is amazing. You mean to tell us that you have actually had sexual intercourse with a ghost?'

Marty smiled apologetically and said, 'Oh, I'm sorry. I thought you said goat!'

★★★

Mark goes to see a psychiatrist. The shrink, in an attempt to analyse him, pulls out some paper and says to Mark, 'I'm going to show

you some inkblots and I want you to tell me
the very first thing that pops into your mind
when you see each one.'

He shows Mark the first drawing and Mark
says, 'Ooooh, hot, dirty sex.'

He gives the same reply for the next inkblot,
and the one after that.

The psychiatrist says, 'Well, you certainly seem
to be a little obsessed with sex.'

Mark replies indignantly, 'Me? You're the
pervert with all the dirty pictures!'

Some women from the IVF support group met
for morning tea to discuss their progress. The
ladies were shocked to discover that one of
their peers who had been on the program for
many years was now six months pregnant.

'Congratulations! Was this from IVF?' gushed
one of the women.

'No, I finally tried a hypnotist,' said the
expectant mum.

'We tried that, but it didn't work,' sighed the
first woman. 'I think Barry and I attended ten
sessions to no avail.'

'See, that's where you're going wrong,' said
the expectant mum in lowered tones, 'you
really need to go *alone.*'

To the Lazy Bastards

Insults

You wouldn't work in an iron lung.

★★★

You wouldn't chew your food if you could digest it another way.

★★★

You wouldn't lift your bum off the chair unless you got bitten.

★★★

Are you working hard or hardly working?

★★★

You're so lazy, you don't walk in your sleep,
you hitchhike.

★★★

Don't just stand there like a cold bottle of piss!

★★★

You wouldn't jump if a shark bit you on the
arse.

★★★

What do you think this is – bush week?

★★★

Quit guffing off!

★★★

Pull your finger out.

★★★

You move slower than a month of Sundays.

★★★

Get a move on, slow coach.

★★★

An honest day's work would take you a whole week.

★★★

Get your arse into gear.

★★★

Changing the TV channel would give you blisters.

★★★

You're a no-hoper.

★★★

When you cark it, they'll bury you in a hammock.

★★★

Your get up and go just got up and went.

★★★

You wouldn't breathe if it didn't happen automatically.

★★★

You wouldn't give up your chair to a fainting paraplegic.

★★★

Jokes

One afternoon, a station manager gets together his ten laziest jackaroos in an attempt to shame them out of their idleness for once and for all.

'Okay, fellas,' he says, 'I have the dead easiest job for the laziest jackaroo on the station. All you've got to do is lie down on a lilo in the watertank, look at girlie magazines and sip on an ice-cold beer. Now, will the laziest bloke please stand forward.'

Quick as a flash, nine men all stand forward. The manager turns to the man left behind and says, 'Now, how come you didn't step forward, Johnno?'

Johnno yawns, 'Aaaah, couldn't be buggered, boss.'

Michelle and Shane find themselves in a bit of financial strife, and sit down to discuss the family budget. The discussion soon becomes rather heated.

'Well, Michelle, if you get off your lazy arse and learn how to cook, then maybe we wouldn't end up getting so much take-away!' rants Shane. 'And, if you bothered to get the vacuum cleaner out once in a while, we wouldn't have to hire a maid to come in twice a week. That's where all our money's going!'

'Oh yeah?' replies Michelle, 'Well, you listen here, Shane. If you bothered to learn how to screw properly, we certainly wouldn't need the gardener, would we?'

★★★

How many men does it take to change a toilet roll?

We don't know, it's never happened.

★★★

Pete was holidaying in Turkey when he stumbled across a beautiful ivory idol in a bazaar. As he was inspecting it for flaws, he was astounded when it suddenly spoke to him: 'Kind sir, I am not really an ivory idol – I am a beautiful princess, and have been trapped in this statue by a wicked witch! All I need is to have sex with someone to break the spell that the witch has cast upon me.'

'Hmmmnnnn ... I might be able to help you out,' replied Pete. 'You see, there's my brother-in-law, Greg, and he's an idle f***ing bastard!'

***

Two unemployed blokes are lining up outside Centrelink having a smoke, waiting for the doors to open so that they could collect their fortnightly allowance.

'Mate,' says one to the other, 'I've heard that over in WA there's a diamond mine where the jewels lay sprawled across the countryside. All you've got to do is bend down and pick the buggers up!'

His mate scornfully replies, 'You've really got to bend down?!'

★★★

What's a man's idea of helping to make the bed?
He gets out of it.

★★★

At the prenatal class, the instructor was teaching women how to breathe correctly. Amid all this huffing and puffing, some of the blokes were looking a little bored.

The instructor turned to them, 'Now, men, you must remember that your partner is not alone in this miracle of life! You have an important part to play, too. One thing you can do to ensure that your ladies are in prime fitness for the birth is walk with them. Just short, gentle bursts are fine. Are there any questions?'

One bloke shyly raises his hand.

'Fire away, sir,' says the instructor.
'Well, when Jenny and I go on this walk, is it okay if she carries the golf bag?'

'I've had it,' said Bob to his mates, 'I'm divorcing that lazy-arse missus of mine! I can stand her dirty ways no longer.'
'Yeah? What happened this time,' yawned his mate.
'I went to piss in the sink this morning, and it was full of dirty dishes!'

Clarry goes to the doctor complaining that he's always tired.
He sighs, 'Doc, my wife asks me to do things around the house, and I just can't cope. I try so hard to mow the lawn, or prune the hedges or even to remove the leaves from the guttering, but I spend most of my time snoozing in my hammock.'
'I see,' replies the doctor. 'Well, in layman's terms, you're a lazy mongrel.'
'Fair enough,' says Clarry, 'but what's the medical term, so I can tell my missus?'

Did you hear about the bloke who didn't bother paying his exorcist?
He was repossessed.

One sunny afternoon old Bert and his mate Cliffy are under a bridge fishing, enjoying a few quiet beers. A funeral procession passes overhead, and Cliffy languidly takes off his hat.

'You know what, Cliffy?' says old Bert, 'You really are a decent fella, taking off your hat like that for a funeral procession.'

'Oh, yeah, I guess so,' shrugs Cliffy. 'But I was married to the old girl for fifty years.'

★★★

To the Bushwhackers

Insults

You bastard from the bush.

***

You geebung.

★★★

So, did they saw off your other head at birth?

★★★

Oi, scrubber!

★★★

Oi, dubbo!

★★★

Oi, bush-pig!

★★★

Jokes

A meeting was held in the town hall regarding the problem of dingoes killing sheep on stations. The local pastoralists thought that poisoning the dingoes was the best way to cull them, whereas the local greenies said that castrating the dingoes was an environmentally friendly option.

'For Christ's sake, you green bastards don't have a bloody clue, do you?' boomed big Jim, one of the station owners. 'The dingoes are killing the sheep, not rooting the mongrels!'

★★★

On a farm in Gippsland lived a chicken and a horse who spent every day playing together. One day, the two were playing when the horse fell into a bog and began to sink. Scared for his life, the horse whinnied for the chicken to go get the farmer for help. Off the chicken ran, back to the farm, clucking frantically all the way.

Arriving at the farm, he searched and searched for the farmer, but to no avail. The farmer had gone to town with the only tractor. Running around, the chicken spied the farmer's new BMW. (Yes, some farmers do manage to make a good living.) The chicken found the keys, picked up a rope and drove back to the bog where the horse was still struggling for its life. The horse was surprised to see the chicken arrive in the shiny BMW, and he managed to get a hold of the loop of rope the chicken tossed to him. After tying the other end to the rear bumper of the farmer's car, the chicken then drove slowly forward and rescued the horse! Happy and proud, the chicken drove the BMW back to the farmhouse, and the farmer was none the wiser when he returned. A few weeks later, after some heavy rain, it was the chicken's turn to fall into the bog, and soon, he too, began to sink.

'Help, horse, help!' he clucked in panic. The horse thought a moment, walked over, and straddled the large bog. Looking underneath, he told the chicken to grab his 'thing' and he would then lift him out. The chicken got a good grip, and the horse pulled him up and out, saving his life.

The moral of the story? When you're hung like a horse, you don't need a BMW to pick up chicks.

★★★

A rich yank was on holiday in Australia and he met up with a farmer named Bluey in the pub. They were discussing farming and the yank asked Bluey how big his farm was. 'Three hundred acres,' was the reply. The yank went on about how he would get in his truck and drive for two days and nights just to get across his farm back home in the States. Bluey's reply was, 'Yeah, I had a truck like that.'

★★★

A farmer in Queensland was giving his blonde wife, Candy, some last-minute instructions before he headed off into town for the day. 'Now, there'll be a vet dropping by this afternoon to artificially inseminate one of the cows. I put a nail by the stall with the cow that I want him to impregnate.'
Satisfied that Candy understood the instructions, the farmer headed off to town. Candy went about her chores all morning, then in the afternoon there was a knock on the door. She opened it to find the vet had arrived to do the artificial insemination. She took him out to the shed and showed him the stall with the nail beside it.
'This is the cow you need to inseminate,' explained Candy.
'And what's the nail for?' asked the vet.

Candy replied, 'I guess that's where you're supposed to hang your pants.'

★★★

The Browns had battled for years on the family farm against drought, flood and fire. One day, Jack Brown junior wins the $15 million Powerball jackpot. Overjoyed, he drives into the city to collect his winnings. Upon returning, he hands a $50 note to his father.

'Here you go, Dad,' he says. 'This is just to say thanks for all that you've done for me over the years.'

'Fifty dollars?!' sputters Jack senior. 'Son, over the years, I've scrimped and saved all to give you a livelihood. I sent you to a good boarding school and let you take over the farm. I don't think you understand how much I struggled, especially early on. Why, I had so little money, that I wasn't even able to make an honest woman out of your mother by marrying her!'

'For God's sake, Dad!' shrieks Jack junior. 'You didn't marry Mum? Well, you know what that makes me!'

'Bloody oath I do. And you're a mean one at that!'

★★★

Heard about the new use they found for sheep in New Zealand?
Wool.

★★★

The drover's wife had spent a few months alone at the station. One day a young swagman turns up at her door asking if he can do some chores for a few meals. Noticing that he had very big feet, the drover's wife decides that this bloke might have a bit of potential 'downstairs', so she welcomes him in for a shower and a feed. After a hot roast and a few beers, they wind up in bed together.

When the swagman awoke the next morning, he found $20 beneath his pillowcase and a note saying, 'Go buy yourself a pair of shoes that fit.'

★★★

A city slicker was zooming through the countryside in his reconditioned MG convertible. As he passes a farm, he is mortified to run over a rooster.

Peeling its sorry carcass off the asphalt, the bloke drives up to the farmhouse with the dead rooster. The farmer's wife answers the door.

'Hello, ma'am,' the city slicker says nervously, 'I'm afraid that I ran over your rooster and now he's dead. I'm so terribly sorry and I do hope that you'll allow me to replace him.'

'Please yourself, mate,' she sighs. 'You'll find the hens waiting out the back.'

★★★

A travelling salesman finds himself stranded out in hicksville. He wearily walks to a nearby farmhouse, whereupon the farmer offers to let him share the guest room with another guest, a 'little redheaded schoolteacher'.

'Oh, terrific,' said the salesman. 'And don't you worry, I'll be a real gentleman.'

'Yeah?' replied the farmer. 'Well, so will the little redheaded schoolteacher.'

★★★

Bushwhacker Etiquette

▌ Dim your headlights for approaching vehicles, even if the gun is loaded and the roos are in sight.

▌ When approaching a stop sign, the vehicle with the biggest bull-bar always has the right of way.

▌ Never tow another ute using pantyhose and sticky tape.

▌ Unlike clothes and shoes, a toothbrush should never be a hand-me-down item.

▌ Do not lay rubber while travelling in a funeral procession.

▌ If you have to vacuum the bed, it's time to change the sheets.

▌ While ears need to be cleaned regularly, this is a job that should be done in private using one's own ute keys.

▌ Plucking unwanted nose hair is time-consuming work. A cigarette lighter and tolerance for pain can accomplish the same goal and save hours.

▌ A centrepiece for the table should never be anything prepared by a taxidermist.

▌ Do not allow the dog to eat at the table – no matter how good his manners are.

▌ If your dog falls in love with a guest's leg, have the decency to leave them alone for a few minutes.

▌ When talking to sheilas, be aggressive. Let her know you are interested: 'I've been wanting to go out with you since I read that stuff on the men's dunny wall two years ago!' is a good opening line.

▌ If a sheila's name does not appear regularly on a dunny wall, odds are good that the date will end in frustration.

▌ When at the movies, refrain from talking to characters on the screen.

▌ Cattle is usually a poor choice for a wedding gift.

▌ It's not okay for the groom to bring a girlfriend to his wedding.

▌ When dancing, never remove your jocks, no matter how hot it is.

▌ A bridal veil made of flyscreen is not only cost effective, but also a proven insect deterrent. For the groom, at least rent a tux. Though uncomfortable, choose socks and shoes over thongs for this special occasion.

▌ Always identify people in your yard before shooting at them.

To the Down and Outs

Insults

You look about as happy as a bastard on
Father's Day.

You don't look too happy mate!

***

You're skint.

***

You're broke.

***

You're as lonely as a bandicoot on a burnt
ridge.

***

You're so broke, you'd lick the paint off the
fence.

***

You're like a broken packet of biscuits.

★★★

You're so skint, you'd wipe with both sides of the dunny-wrap.

★★★

If you laughed your face would crack.

★★★

Things are crook in Musselbrook.

★★★

You're on a damp squib.

★★★

You're as happy as a boxing kangaroo in a fog.

★★★

You're so broke, you'd eat the chewing gum off your enemy's boot.

★★★

You're a blue-nosed wowser.

★★★

You've got the rough end of the pineapple.

★★★

You're as mopey as a wet hen.

★★★

You haven't got a bean.

★★★

You haven't got a brass razoo.

★★★

You haven't got a cracker, Polly.

★★★

You're stumped up.

★★★

You're stony broke.

★★★

You're so broke, you'd steal the paper out of a public dunny.

★★★

You're as miserable as a bandicoot.

★★★

You're so skint, burglars break into your house and leave money.

★★★

If it were raining palaces, you'd be hit on the head by a dunny door.

★★★

You don't have a pot to piss in.

★★★

If you bought a kangaroo it wouldn't hop.

★★★

You'd eat a horse and chase the donkey.

★★★

If it were raining virgins, you'd be locked in the dunny with a poofter.

★★★

If you were eating a pear and swallowed the seeds, you'd grow a tree out of your nostrils.

★★★

You're so skint, you'd wave around an icy-pole and call it air-conditioning.

★★★

If you were eating a lamington, you'd inhale some desiccated coconut and cark it.

★★★

You'd chase garbage trucks with a shopping list in your hand.

★★★

You'd stand outside Kentucky Fried Chicken and lick other people's fingers.

★★★

You're so skint, you'd eat Weet-bix with a fork to save milk.

Jokes

A rich guy and a poor guy were talking about what they were getting their wives for Christmas. The rich guy said, 'I'm getting Anastasia a fur coat and a BMW. If she doesn't like the coat, she can return it to the store in the car.'

'Wow,' said the poor guy. 'She'll love those gifts. I've got my wife a silk blouse and a vibrator.'

'A vibrator!' exclaimed the rich guy.

'Yep,' replied the poor guy. 'That way, if she doesn't like the blouse she can go f*** herself.'

★★★

Mick's a bit down on his luck, so decides to go into a bar and orders himself a beer. He spots two women at the other end of the bar and orders them a round of drinks, too.

'Hey, Mick, don't waste your money,' said the bartender. 'Those two are lesbians.'

Mick replies, 'Hey, no worries, buy them a drink and put it on my tab.'

After he finishes his beer he says to the bartender, 'Another beer for me and another round for the girls.'

'You're wasting your money, Mick, I'm telling you, those chicks are lesbians.'

'Aw, what's a thing like that matter? Get them another drink and add it to my tab.'

This continues for three more rounds and finally, with beer-induced confidence, Mick brushes his hand through his hair, clears his throat and walks over to the ladies.

He suavely pulls up a chair, smiles and says, 'So, ladies, which part of Lesbia are you from?'

★★★

A down and out young man scored a date with the girl of his dreams, and wanting to impress her, he decided to take her out to a really expensive French restaurant. Alas, he couldn't read a word of French, but rather than admit this to her he went ahead and selected a dish for himself. The waiter sniggered when he ordered his meal, but brought it nevertheless: a whole pig – including the head – smothered in barbecue sauce.

When the waiter wheeled it over, the poor young man was mortified, but he didn't bat an eyelid. Reaching into the pig's mouth, he took out the red apple.

'I know it's extravagant,' he told his date, 'but this is the only way I like fruit.'

★★★

The lady of the house summons her butler to the parlour.
'Now, Jeeves, I demand that you unzip my dress!'
Flushing a deep beetroot-red, Jeeves does as he is told.
'Now, Jeeves, I demand that you peel off my stockings!'
Again, Jeeves does as he is told.
'Now, Jeeves, I demand that you take off my underwear – and should I catch you in my clothing again, you will be instantly dismissed!'

★★★

A bloke walks up to his brand new Subaru WRX in the Safeway car park and is mortified to discover that his bonnet is entirely crumpled. Beneath the windscreen wiper is a note that reads:
"Mate, I'm sorry that I pranged your new car. The simple fact is that I was backing out and didn't look where I was going. Plenty of witnesses seemed impressed that I wrote

down my details. But the funny thing is ... I didn't."

★★★

Bluey was a bit down on his luck. He'd lost the farm and now his missus had died. So he went down to the local newspaper to place a death notice. As he was low on cash, he simply wrote: *Betty's dead*.

'Betty's dead!' exclaimed the clerk. 'That's a bit harsh – after all, you were married to the woman for thirty-five years. You know Bluey, you're able to get a five-word notice for the amount you've paid. Go on, get your money's worth.'

'Fair enough,' mumbled Bluey. 'Let's try: *Betty's dead: Holden for sale.*'

★★★

Polva was in Communist Moscow doing her weekly shopping. She went to the bakery, but as there was such a long queue she decided to walk on. The queue at the butcher store was even longer so instead she tried the grocery store, where the queue was even longer than the bakery and butcher queues put together.

'I've had enough of this,' she huffed in frustration.

Grabbing her husband's gun, she decided to

march down to the Kremlin and do away with
the Secretary General. But when she got there
she found 200 people in line before her.

***

There were two people walking down the
street. One was an artist. The other one didn't
have a job either.

***

A photographer from an environmental
magazine was assigned to cover a fire that had
broken out in the Hattah National Park. The
magazine wanted to show the havoc the fire
was creating and the damage it was doing to
the trees.

By the time the photographer had taken a
plane to Mildura and hired a car to take him
closer to the area, it was quite late and he
knew he'd better move fast or he wouldn't be
able to shoot anything.

He hurried onto the small strip runway where
a small plane had been arranged to take him
over the burning area. He saw a plane
warming up, and grabbing his bag, he rushed
on, shouting, 'Okay, let's go!'

The pilot swung the little plane into the wind
and within minutes they were in the air. The

photographer said, 'Fly over the park and take two or three low passes so I can take some pictures.'

'Why?' asked the pilot.

'Because I'm a photographer,' he snapped, 'and photographers take photographs!'

The pilot was silent for a moment. Finally, he stammered, 'You mean you're not the flight instructor?'

***

The doctor had just informed his patient that he had only three minutes left to live.

Absolutely stunned, the patient wailed, 'Why me?! Only three minutes! Why is life so unfair? Doc, surely there must be something you can do for me!'

'Well,' replied the doctor, 'I guess I could boil you an egg.'

***

To Someone Who Doesn't Belong

Insults

You're all alone like a country dunny.

***

You're like a lily on a dustbin.

***

You're a Scotty Neville. (Scott no friends and Neville will!)

***

You're like a one-legged man at an arse-kicker's picnic.

★★★

You're like a pickpocket at a nudist camp.

★★★

You're like a pork sandwich at a bar mitzvah.

★★★

You're like a shag on a rock.

★★★

You'd be better off drinking with the flies.

★★★

You're like a spare prick at a wedding.

★★★

You're like a tailor at a nudist camp.

★★★

You're like a laundromat at a nudist camp.

★★★

You're on your Pat Malone.

★★★

Jokes

Three married couples die in a terrible train wreck and promptly arrive at the pearly gates. St Peter greets them with his clipboard and asks for their names.

'St Peter, I'm so honoured to meet you!' says the first man, 'My name is Arthur Jones and this is my wife, Brandy.'

'Well, it's nice to meet you, too, Arthur!' smiles Peter. 'But I'm afraid I have some bad news. I can't admit anyone with a name connected to alcohol. You are welcome to come in, but Brandy's got to go.'

Dejectedly, Arthur and Brandy shuffle 'downstairs' to Hell.

The next man in line says, 'Hi there, St Peter, my name is Barney Keizer and this is my wife, Penny.'

Shaking his head, St Peter says to Barney and his wife, 'I'm afraid that I cannot allow anyone with a name connected to money into Heaven. Sorry, but you've got to go downstairs, too, Penny.'

Overhearing all this, the third man in line

turns to his wife and says, 'Fanny, I think we might have a problem.'

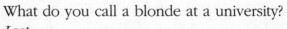

What do you call a blonde at a university?
Lost.

★★★

At a job interview, the HR officer asked a candidate if she had any special skills and talents.

'Well,' she replied, 'I'm very good at doing crosswords and writing catchy slogans in 25 words or less for magazine competitions.'

'That's great,' replied the HR officer, 'but I was

more so thinking of special skills and talents in the workplace.'
'But those talents *are* in the workplace,' replied the applicant.

★★★

The elder priest, speaking to the younger priest, said, 'Um, listen, I need to discuss something with you. Now, I know you were reaching out to the young people when you put comfortable recliners in to replace the first four pews. It worked. We got the front of the church filled first; that was a good plan.'
The young priest smiled and nodded, 'Thank you, Father.'

The old one continued, 'And, you told me a little more beat to the music would bring young people back to church, so I supported you when you brought in that rock and roll gospel choir that packed us to the balcony.'

'So,' said the younger priest, 'what's the problem then?'

'Well,' said the elder priest, 'I'm afraid you've gone too far with the drive-thru confessional.'

'But Father,' protests the young priest. 'My confessions have nearly doubled since I began that!'

'I know, my son, but the flashing "Toot 'n' Tell or Go to Hell" neon pink sign really has to go.'

★★★

A bloke from New Zealand wandered into a fish and chip shop in Glenelg and ordered some 'fush and chups please, buddy'.

'A-ha! You're a bloody Kiwi, aren't ya?' exclaimed the chipper.

This set the Kiwi off. He had absolutely had it with being ridiculed about how he spoke, so he took some elocution lessons to lose his accent.

Twelve months later, he walked back into the shop and asked with a nasal Aussie twang, 'I'll have some fish 'n' chips please, cobber.'

'You're a bloody Kiwi, aren't ya?' exclaimed the proprietor.

'And what makes you say that?' sighed the

Kiwi, wondering if he'd gone too far with the
'cobber' add-in.
'Well, this joint has been a tattoo parlour for
the past six months.'

***

A man was travelling the world, and one day
happened upon a group of natives who
invited him to become a member of their
tribe.
'To do so,' explained the leader of the tribe,
'you've got to drink five litres of seal blood,
wrestle a polar bear, and have sex with a
woman from the tribe.'
Anxious to become a member of the tribe, the
man agreed and set out to complete his tasks.
Several hours went by, and the natives were
wondering what had happened to him. Finally
the man returned, covered in blood and with
his clothes torn.
'Well,' he boasted, 'I did it! I finished two of
my tasks. Now just tell me where to find that
woman you want me to wrestle.'

***

A spaceship landed next to a service station
and the captain sent his first officer out to
interview some of the Earthlings.
The first officer went up to a petrol pump and
said, 'Take me to your leader.'

Not surprisingly, the petrol pump didn't respond.

Back on the spaceship, the first officer told his captain that the Earthlings wouldn't talk, they just stood there with a silly look on their faces and their dicks stuck in their ears.

***

A deeply depressed young woman was contemplating throwing herself off the Sydney Harbour Bridge. She walked around Circular Quay on her way toward the bridge when she came across a suave-looking sailor. They got into a conversation, and he managed to talk her out of committing suicide. Using his sea-dog charms, the sailor also persuaded the young woman to stow away aboard his cruise liner to Rio.

The young woman decided that this was a much better option to killing herself, and climbed on board. She hid in a lifeboat aboard the ship, and, every night, the sailor brought her food and drink and they made glorious love until dawn.

Finally, after six weeks, she was discovered by the captain of the ship.

'Oi, missy! What are you doing hiding in that lifeboat?' he demanded.

'It's no problem,' she smirked. 'You see, I have an arrangement with one of the sailors. He's taking me to raunchy Rio, and, what's more, he's screwing me stupid.'

'You bloody bet he is, love!' came the reply, 'This is the Manly Ferry!'

★★★

At the cinema, an usher noticed a man stretched across four seats. 'I'm sorry, sir, but you're only allowed to have one seat.'

The man didn't budge, so the usher tried again. 'Sir, if you don't move, I'll have to get the manager.'

But again, the man didn't budge. Furious, the usher went to get the manager, who similarly was not able to get the man to move. He had no choice but to call the police. A policeman arrived in no time and looked down at the guy, still stretched across four seats.

'What's yer name, bud?'
The man mumbled, 'Paul.'
'And where are you from, Paul?'
'The balcony.'

To the Gung-ho Gamblers

Insults

You'd bet on two flies walking up the wall.

You'd bet on the number of daisies growing on your mother's grave.

You'd bet on how much fur your cat would lose over summer.

You'd bet on the number of beers a pub would go through on Melbourne Cup day.

Jokes

It was early in the morning at Jupiter's Casino, and a gorgeous woman walked over to one of the craps tables where two dealers were standing bored and waiting for custom. She said that she had money to burn, and wanted to bet fifty thousand dollars on a single roll of the dice.

'Sure thing, lady,' replied one of the dealers, smirking at the other.

'Great,' she cooed, 'however, I will do this on one condition. You must allow me to remove my skirt and underpants before I roll the dice.' The dealers were both dumbfounded, so stunned that they could barely nod their heads in the affirmative.

Once she had ascertained their answer, the woman whipped off her skirt and undies as quick as a flash and rolled the dice.

'Woo hoo! I've won!' she squealed, scooping up the chips and streaking out the door.

The two dealers stood there in gobsmacked silence.

'So, what did she roll, anyway,' said one of the

dealers to the other (as soon as he could remember how to speak).

'Crikey, I don't know!' came the reply. 'I thought you were watching the dice!'

★★★

Reg's wife is pregnant with twins, and with this birth they'll have eight children. Already down on his luck, Reg goes into the bank requesting a loan. After his application is rejected, Reg books an appointment with the bank manager.

After giving Reg a lengthy sermon on the importance of saving, and admonishing him for having an abysmal record when it comes to putting money away, the bank manager tells Reg that he is simply too much of a risk to the bank.

In tears, Reg pleads with the bank manager, 'Sir, you don't know how much I need this loan for my wife and all of our kids! We've already got six of the little buggers, and there's another two on the way. I promise you that I'll pay you back in a timely manner, I really promise!'

'Hmmnnn ... how about if you take on an extra job?' says the bank manager, 'Are you willing to do that?'

'Well, sir, I already have two jobs, working both nightshift and dayshift, but I'll certainly

find yet another job if that's what it will take.'
'Okay. Well, I'll give you the loan if you take on another job. However, you must do another thing. Tell me, which of my eyes is made of glass?'
After a great deal of thought Reg responds, 'Your left eye.'
'My left eye! Well, that's correct, Reg!' smiles the bank manager. 'Most people tend to choose my right eye. Tell me, how did you guess?'
'Well, your left eye looked remotely human.'

★★★

Heard about the Irish lottery?
If you win you get $10 a year over a million years.

★★★

A man walked into a cafe and said to the waitress, 'My name is Brodie, and I have a proposition for you. I'll bet $10,000 to your $100 that by this time tomorrow your nipples will have disappeared.'
The waitress was shocked, but her wages were pretty pathetic so she thought she'd give it a go.
'Okay, you're on,' she said.
The two shook hands and the man left, promising to meet her the next day.

For the rest of the day the waitress was ultra paranoid about her breasts. She bandaged them up to protect them. She kept away from all sharp objects. She even had a cold shower just to ensure that she wouldn't burn her nipples.

The next day Brodie returned to the cafe where the waitress worked, this time accompanied by a businessman. Brodie walked up to the waitress and said, 'Well?'

With a triumphant expression, the waitress tore open her blouse and flashed her tits at Brodie and the businessman. The nipples were still there, normal as ever.

The businessman gasped and fell to the floor. Brodie handed the waitress $10,000 then bent down and reached into the businessman's pocket.

'What's the story?' asked the waitress, motioning to the businessman.

'Easy,' said Brodie. 'I bet him $50,000 that I could walk in here and have you flash your tits at me.'

How do poker champs find out they're sacked?
They get discarded.

One day a bloke is at the casino playing the one-armed bandits when he notices a frog sitting next to him. 'Ribbit,' says the frog, 'use this machine.'

A little weirded out, the man nevertheless swaps machines, and what do you know, with just one sweep of the lever, he lands the $25,000 jackpot.

The frog then says, 'Ribbit, mister, why don't you use the machine over there?'

And so the man goes over to the machine and sits down. Straight away the golden dollars are flooding out. The man is now positively loaded.

Being a little greedy, but, hey, you can't string him up for that, the man decides to take the frog to where the big bucks are at, Las Vegas, Nevada.

So, he buys a ticket for both himself and the frog, and they fly out that very evening.

Once in Las Vegas, the man is playing a poker machine recommended by the frog. What do you know, he hits the five-million-dollar jackpot.

Beside himself, he turns to the frog and says, 'Frog, you've made me a millionaire, and a very happy man. How can I ever repay you?'

Luring the man back into the hotel room, the frog replies, 'Ribbit, ribbit. Well, you could kiss me to start.'

The man figures that he really does owe the frog. So, he bends down and gives the frog a big sloppy kiss. Magically, the frog transforms into a beautiful 16-year-old girl.

'And that, your honour, is how the girl ended up in my room ...'

Joelie said to her friend, 'My grandpa doesn't drink, smoke, gamble, eat fatty foods or even swear. We're all going to celebrate his ninety-fifth birthday tomorrow.'

Todd looked at her, smirking, and asked, 'How?'

A young fella at the construction site was bragging that he could outdo anyone in a feat of strength. He made a special case of making fun of Morris, one of the older workmen. Morris had finally had enough.

'Why don't you put your money where your mouth is?' he said. 'I will bet a week's wages that I can haul something in a wheelbarrow over to that building that you won't be able to wheel back.'

'You're on, old man,' the young buck replied. 'It's a bet! Let's see what you got.'

Morris reached out and grabbed the
wheelbarrow by the handles. Then, nodding
to the young bloke, he said, 'All right. Get in.'

***

A blonde busily fed coins into a vending
machine laughing with glee as each Coke can
rolled out the bottom.
After patiently waiting for a minute or so, the
man waiting behind her angrily sighed, 'For
God's sake, this is ridiculous. How much
longer are you going to be?'
'You'll just have to hold your horses!' hissed
the blonde, 'Can't you see that I'm on a
winning streak!'

***

It is the end of term and young Charles is on the train riding home from his boarding residences at Geelong Grammar. He finds himself seated next to a bunch of blokes from the Ford plant.

A foreman named Gazza turns to Charles and says, 'Hey, mate! We're having a general knowledge quiz here. Do you want to join us?'

'Well, why not?' says Charles. 'But I must warn you; I am well on my way to becoming dux of the school and general knowledge is my strong point.'

'Fair enough,' says Gazza. 'To make things fair considering your brainy advantage, how about we pay you five bucks for every correct answer, and you pay us ten?'

Charles agrees that this sounds fair.

'Right,' smiles Gazza, 'tell me, what insect has four eyes, eight legs, and can only fly backwards?'

Charles is flabbergasted to find himself stumped. With a great deal of embarrassment, he hands over his ten dollars.

'You know chaps, I'm afraid that I have no idea. What insect has four eyes, eight legs and can only fly backwards?'

Gazza grins, 'Buggered if I know, mate, but here's your five bucks.'

Bert the publican is known as a man who can
never turn down a bet. After downing a fair
bit of amber fluid, Nick (one of his regulars)
says to him, 'Hey Bert! I bet you fifty bucks
that I can urinate in a VB stubby as you slide
it along the bar, all without spilling a single
drop.'

Without batting an eyelid, Bert replies, 'You're
on, Nick!'

So Nick unzips his trousers and aims as Bert
slides a VB stubby along the bar. Not
surprisingly, Nick makes a total mess of the
bar.

'You're a bloody pathetic marksman,' smirks
Bert, 'hand over the fifty!'

'Fair enough,' laughs Nick. 'But I'm the winner
here. Those six blokes over by the pool table

said they'd give me fifty bucks each if I
managed to piss all over your bar and get
away with it!'

To Other Aussies

Insults

You sheep shagger.

***

You sheila.

★★★

You wanker.

★★★

You tugger.

★★★

You fly-swatter.

★★★

You tosser.

★★★

You Toorak tart.

★★★

You brain-dead petrol sniffer.

★★★

You country bumpkin.

★★★

You mullet head.

★★★

Jokes

An Australian, an Irishman and an Englishman are sitting in a bar. There is only one other person in the bar: a bloke sitting in a corner. The three men keep looking at the bloke, trying to think who he is because he seems terribly familiar. They stare and stare, wondering where they have seen him before. Suddenly, the Irishman cries out, 'My God! I know that man! It's Jesus!'

The others look again and find that their Irish friend is right – it is indeed the one and only Jesus.

The Irishman calls out across the lounge, 'Hey! Hey, you! Are you Jesus?'

Jesus looks over at him, smiles a small smile and nods his head.

'Yes, I am Jesus,' he says.

The Irishman calls the bartender over and says to him, 'I'd like you to give Jesus over there a Guinness from me.'

The bartender pours Jesus a Guinness. Jesus looks over, raises his glass, thanks them and drinks.

The Englishman then calls out, 'So, you're Jesus are you, sir?'

Jesus smiles and says, 'Yes, I am Jesus.'

The Englishman beckons the bartender and tells him to send over a pint of Stone's Green Ginger Wine for Jesus, which the bartender duly does. As before, Jesus accepts the drink and smiles over at the table.

Then the Australian calls out, 'Oi, you! D'ya reckon you're Jesus or what?'

Jesus nods and says, 'Yes, I am Jesus.'

The Australian is most impressed and has the bartender send over some Vic Bitter for Jesus, who accepts it gracefully.

Some time later, after finishing the drinks, Jesus leaves his seat and approaches the three friends. He reaches for the hand of the Irishman and shakes it thanking him for the Guinness.

When he lets go, the Irishman gives a cry of amazement, 'Oh God! The arthritis is gone! The arthritis I've had for years is gone! It's a miracle!'

Jesus then shakes the Englishman's hand, thanking him for the ginger wine.

Upon letting go, the Englishman's eyes widen in shock, 'By Jove, my nervous twitch! The twitch I've had for 40 years is completely gone! It's a miracle!'

Jesus then goes to approach the Australian who says, 'Back off, mate! I'm on worker's compensation!'

★★★

What's the difference between an Aussie wedding and an Aussie funeral?
There's one less drunk at the funeral.

★★★

'Paul, you'd better prepare yourself,' said the doctor. 'I've got some bad news for you.'
'What, doc, what is it?'
'Paul, I'm so sorry to tell you this, but you've only got six months to live.'
'Six months!' cried Paul. 'My God, what am I going to do?'

The doctor shrugged. 'Paul, if I were you, I'd get married and move to Canberra. It'll be the longest six months of your life.'

★★★

In some remote parts, 'Tie Me Kangaroo Down, Sport' is known as a drover's love song.

★★★

An Aussie, a New Zealander and a Canadian were all in Saudi Arabia, sharing a smuggled carton of beer. All of a sudden, Saudi police rushed in and arrested them. The mere possession of alcohol is a severe offence there, so for the terrible crime of actually being caught consuming the beer they were sentenced to death.

However, after many months and with the help of some very good lawyers, the three poor fellows were able to successfully appeal their sentence down to life imprisonment. By a stroke of luck, it was a Saudi national holiday the day their trial finished, and the extremely benevolent sheikh decided they could be released after receiving just 20 lashes each of the whip.

As they were preparing for their punishment, the sheikh suddenly said, 'It's my first wife's birthday today, and she has asked me to allow each of you one wish before your whipping.' The Canadian was first in line, so he thought about this for a while and then said, 'Please tie a pillow to my back.'

This was done, but the pillow only lasted 10 lashes before the whip went through.

The Kiwi was next up, and after watching the scene, said, 'Please fix two pillows on my back.'

But even two pillows could only take 15

lashes before the whip went through again. The Aussie was the last one up, but before he could say anything, the sheikh turned to him and said, 'You are from a most beautiful country, your cricket team is the best in the world, your footballers are terrific and your women are very sexy. For this, you may have two wishes!'

'Thanks, mate, your Most Royal and Merciful Highness,' the Aussie replies. 'In recognition of your kindness, my first wish is that you give me not 20, but 100 lashes.'

'Not only are you an honourable, handsome and powerful man, you are also very brave,' says the sheikh, with an admiring look on his face. 'If 100 lashes is what you desire, then so be it. And your second wish? What is that to be?' the sheikh asks.

'Please tie the Kiwi to my back.'

In Australia, a gentleman is he who gets out of the shower to piss in the sink.

A migrant went for a job and was told he would have to pass an IQ test. When he asked what an IQ was the employer explained that anyone with an IQ of 100 would be admitted to university, but a bloke with an IQ of 50 wouldn't be able to tie up his shoelaces.

'Oh,' said the migrant. 'So that's why so many Australians wear thongs.'

***

A bunch of touring Aussie rugby players are out and about seeing the sights of Dublin. The tour guide announces, 'And to your right, we are passing the biggest pub in Ireland!'
The burliest bloke from down the back yells out, 'And why aren't we stopping?'

Lucinda is driving through outback Australia on her way back to the city from a sales conference when she sees another woman thumbing for a ride on the side of the road. As the trip had been long and quiet, and she feels like a bit of company, Lucinda stops the car.
The hitch-hiker gets in and introduces herself as May from Broome.
After a bit of small talk, May notices a brown bag on the front seat. 'What's in the bag?' she asks.
'It's a bottle of wine. I got it for my husband,' replies Lucinda.
May is silent for a moment then says, 'Good trade.'

Some Handy Facts About Australians

1. The bigger the hat, the smaller the
    farm.

All mine!

2. The shorter the nickname, the more
    popular you are.
3. There is no Australian event that cannot
    be improved by a sausage sizzle.
4. If the guy next to you is swearing like a
    wharfie he's probably a media billionaire.
    Or, on the other hand, he may be a
    wharfie.

5. There is no food that cannot be improved by the application of tomato sauce.

6. On the beach, all Australians hide their keys and wallets by placing them inside their shoes. No thief has ever worked this out.

7. Industrial design knows of no article more useful than the plastic milk-crate.

8. All our best heroes are losers or murderers.

9. The alpha male in any group is he who takes the barbecue tongs from the hands of the host and blithely begins turning the snags.

10. It's not summer until the steering wheel is too hot to hold.

11. A thong is not a piece of scanty underwear, as in America, but a fine example of Australian footwear. A group of sheilas wearing black rubber thongs may not be as exciting as you had hoped.

12. It is proper to refer to your best mate as 'a total bastard'.

13. Historians believe the widespread use of the word 'mate' can be traced to the harsh conditions on the Australian frontier in the 1890s, and the development of a code of mutual aid, or 'mateship'. Alternatively, Australians may just be really hopeless with remembering people's names.

14. If you can't stomach a good slathering of Vegemite on toast, you're just not true blue.

15. If it can't be fixed with pantyhose and fencing wire, it's not worth fixing.

16. The most popular and widely praised family in any street is the one that has the biggest swimming pool.

17. It's considered better to be down on your luck than up yourself.

18. The phrase 'we've got a great lifestyle' means everyone in the family drinks too much.

19. If invited to a party, you should take cheap red wine and then spend all night drinking the host's beer. (Don't worry, he'll have catered for it.)

20. If there is any sort of free event or party within 100 kilometres, you'd be a mug not to go.

21. The phrase 'a simple picnic' is not known. You should take everything in your fridge and kitchen cupboards. If you don't need to make three trips back to the car, you're not trying.

22. Unless you're ethnic, you are not permitted to sit down in your front yard, or on your front porch. Pottering about, gardening or leaning on the fence is acceptable. Just don't sit; that's what backyards are for.

23. On picnics, the esky is always too small, creating a food-versus-grog battle that can only ever be resolved by leaving the salad at home.

24. When on a country holiday, the neon sign advertising the motel's pool will always be larger than the pool itself.

25. The men are tough, but the women are tougher.

26. One of the truest Australian experiences is burning your bare feet on asphalt as you run to the milk bar on a hot summer's day

to get some ciggies.

27. The chief test of manhood is one's ability to install a beach umbrella in high winds.

28. Australians love new technology. Years after their introduction, most conversations on mobile phones are principally about the fact that the call is 'being made on my mobile'.

29. There comes a time in every Australian's life when he/she realises that Aerogard is worse than the flies.

30. And, finally, don't let the tourist books fool you. No one ever says 'cobber' to anyone ... ever!

★★★

Aussie National Address

We, the people of the broad brown land of Oz, wish to be recognised as a free nation of sheilas and blokes. We come from many lands (although a few too many of us come from New Zealand) and, although we live in the best country in the world, we reserve the right to bitch and moan about it whenever we bloody like.

We are a nation divided into many states. First, there's Victoria, named after a queen who didn't believe in lesbians. Victoria is the realm of turtlenecks, cafe latte, grand final day and big horse races. Its capital is Melbourne, whose chief marketing-pitch is that it's 'livable'. At least, that's what they think. The rest of us think it is too bloody cold and wet. Next, there's New South Wales, the realm of pastel shorts, fluffy cappuccino with sugar, thin books read quickly, and millions of dancing queens. Its capital Sydney has more queens than any other city in the world, and is proud of it. Its mascots are Bondi lifesavers who pull their Speedos up their cracks to keep the left and right sides of their brains separate.

Down south we have the often forgotten Tasmania, a state based on the notion that the family that bonks together stays together. In Tassie, everyone gets an extra chromosome at conception. Maps of the state bring smiles to the sternest faces – that is, when we remember to tack it on.

South Australia is the province of half-decent reds, a festival of foreigners and bizarre axe-murders. South Australia is the state of innovation; where else can you so effectively reuse country bank vaults and barrels as in Snowtown? They had the Grand Prix, but lost it when the views of Adelaide (also named after a queen) sent the Formula One drivers to sleep at the wheel.

Western Australia is too far from anywhere to be relevant in this document. It's main claim to fame is that it doesn't have daylight savings because if it did all the men would get erections on the bus on the way to work. WA was the last state to stop importing convicts, and many of them still work there as 'entrepreneurs'.

The Northern Territory is the red heart of our land. Outback plains, sheep stations the size of Europe, kangaroos, jackaroos, emus, Uluru and dusty kids with big smiles. It also has the highest beer consumption of anywhere on the planet, and its creek beds have the highest aluminium content of anywhere, too. Although the Territory is the centrepiece of our national culture, few of us live there, and the rest prefer to fly over it on our way to Bali.

And there's Queensland. While any mention of God seems silly in a document defining a nation of half-arsed agnostics, it is worth noting that God probably made Queensland. Why he filled it with dickheads remains a mystery ...

Oh yes, and there's Canberra. The nation's capital. The least said about that, the better. We, the citizens of Oz, are united by the Pacific Highway, whose treacherous twists and turns kill more of us each year than die by murder.

We are united in our lust for international recognition, so desperate for praise we leap in joy when a gaggle of corrupt IOC officials tells us that Sydney is better than Beijing. We are united by a democracy so flawed that a political party, albeit a redneck gun-toting one, can get a million votes and still not win one seat in Federal Parliament; however, Brian bloody Harradine can get 24,000 votes and run the whole country.

Not that we're whingeing, we leave that to our Pommy immigrants. We want to make: 'No worries, mate,' our national phrase; 'She'll be right, mate,' our national attitude; and 'Waltzing Matilda' our national anthem (so what if it's about a sheep-stealing crim who tops himself).

We love sport so much, our newsreaders can read the death toll from a sailing race and still tell us who's winning in the same breath. And we're the best in the world at all the sports that count, like cricket, netball, rugby, AFL, roo-shooting, two-up and horseracing.

We also have the biggest rock, the tastiest pies, and the worst-dressed Olympians in the known universe. We don't know much about art, but we know we hate the bloody poofs who make it.

We shoot, we vote. We are girt by sea and pissed by lunchtime. And even though we might seem a racist, closed-minded, sports-obsessed little people, at least we're better than those f***ing Kiwis.

To Religious Zealots

Insults

You amen-snorter.

You Bible-basher.

***

You God-botherer.

★★★

You bloomin' sky pilot!

★★★

You oughta be called Reverend Chester (the child molester).

★★★

Jokes

One day, in the warm, tropical waters of the Caribbean, two prawns were swimming around. One was called John and the other was called Christian. The prawns were constantly being harassed and threatened by sharks that patrolled the area.

Finally, one day during a tropical storm, John said to Christian, 'I'm bored and frustrated at being a prawn. I wish I was a big, fierce shark, then I wouldn't have any worries about being eaten.'

Just as John said this, he was struck by lightning – and the oddest thing happened. He immediately turned into a shark! Horrified, Christian hurriedly swam away, afraid of being eaten by his old mate.

Time went on and John found himself becoming bored and lonely as a shark. All his old mates simply swam away whenever he came close to them. John didn't realise that his new menacing appearance was the cause of his sad plight.

During the next tropical storm, John figured that the same lightning force could change

him back into a prawn. Lightning never strikes
twice except in stories like these, but while he
was thinking of being a prawn, a flash of
lightning struck the water next to John and, lo
and behold, he turned back into prawn.
With tears of joy in his tiny little eyes, John
swam back to his friends and bought them all
a drink. Looking around the gathering at the
reef, he searched for his old pal.
'Where's Christian?' he asked.
'He's at home, distraught that his best friend
changed sides to the enemy and became a
shark,' came the reply from one of the
prawns.

Eager to put things right again and end the
mental pain and torture, he set off to
Christian's house. As he opened the coral gate,

the memories came flooding back. He banged on the door and shouted, 'It's me, John, your old friend, come out and see me again.'

Christian replied, 'Hey, no way, man, you'll eat me. You're a shark, the enemy, and I'll not be tricked by the likes of you.'

John cried back, 'No, I'm not. That was the old me. I've changed ...'

(Wait for it.)

'... I'm a prawn again, Christian.'

★★★

Two Jewish guys were seated together on a flight from Sydney to Melbourne. They'd been in the air for about half an hour when the younger man asked the other if he had the time. There was no answer. So he tried again. 'Can you tell me the time, please?' But again there was no answer.

It wasn't until the aeroplane was descending that the old man quickly looked at his watch and said it was midday.

The young man asked, perplexed, 'Well, why on Earth didn't you tell me the time earlier?'

'Well, you know what it's like,' began the man. 'People get talking to each other in situations like these. We could become friends, especially as we are both Jewish. I'd be obliged to invite you home for dinner. I have a lovely daughter and you are a handsome

young man. Romance could blossom and
before long you could be asking for her hand
in marriage. And, to put it bluntly, I don't
want no son-in-law who hasn't got a watch.'

★★★

Jake, the local wannabe comedian, was in
good form at the pub one Saturday night.
'Right, so the bus stops and these two Jews
get off ...' he began.
Suddenly, a bloke gets off his stool and
protests, 'Look, mate, I'm Jewish and I'm sick
and tired of hearing about two Jews doing this
and two Jews doing that. Pick on some other
mob for a change.'
'Okay,' said Jake, 'point taken.'
So he starts again: 'The bus stops and these
two Aborigines get off and one said, "So there
we were at my son's bar mitzvah ...'

★★★

Kneeling unsteadily on the floor, an old black
preacher, who was dying, took his Bible and
prayed to God.
'Almighty God,' he said, 'I have been your
faithful servant all my life. I am now almost on
my deathbed, and I ask you – nay, I beg you
– just to answer me one question. God, are
you black or are you white?'
Suddenly, the room darkened, a flash of light

burst into the room, and a voice boomed out, 'I am what I am.'

The preacher's brow knotted, 'Please, Lord, that's no answer. I need to know!'

The voice boomed again, 'Dummy! If I were black I would have said unto Moses and now unto you, "I be what I be."'

∗∗∗

After doing her shopping for the crippled old people at the convent, the nun got into her car and drove a few kilometres before running out of petrol. Luckily, a passing motorist stopped to see if he could help.

'I just need some fuel,' said the nun.

'Well, I can give you some petrol, but I don't have anything to put it in,' said the man. Remembering that she had a bedpan in the back seat of her car, the nun went to get it, and in no time at all the man had siphoned enough petrol from his tank to get her to the nearest petrol station. As she began to fill her car up from the bedpan, he waved goodbye and zoomed off.

Just then another motorist drove by. Seeing what the nun was doing, the man said to his passenger, 'Now that's what I call faith!'

A young pastor, who normally rode a bike, was walking gloomily down the street when he came upon an older pastor. The older pastor could see his young friend was deeply troubled.

'What is bothering you, my son?' he asked.

'Well, it appears a member of my congregation has stolen my bike,' he replied sadly.

The elder said, 'If I may give you some advice you might get your bike back. Next Sunday morning during your sermon, preach about the Ten Commandments, and when you get to "Thou shall not steal" really emphasise it.'

The next week the two pastors met again, and this time the young pastor was riding his bike.

'Well,' said the older one, 'I see my advice worked.'

'Yes,' the young one replied, 'I took your advice and preached on the Ten Commandments and when I got to "Thou shall not commit adultery" I remembered where I left my bike.'

★★★

It was the start of the school year and the nun introduced herself to her new grade three class. She went around to each of her new students, asking them what they wanted to be when they grew up.

'I'm gonna be a doctor,' yelled Dave.

'I'm gonna be a firefighter,' squealed Tamsin.

'I'm gonna be a florist,' smiled Carrie.

'I'm gonna be a prostitute!' bellowed Sarah.

The nun passed out upon hearing Sarah's desired career, and when she came to she found the children gathered around, looking at her with concern.

'Sarah, Sarah, wh-wh-what did you say you wanted to be?' spluttered the nun.

'A prostitute,' she repeated.

Sitting up and breathing a sigh of relief, the nun smiled, 'Praise the Lord. I thought you said "Protestant".'

An atheist was spending a quiet day fishing when suddenly his boat is attacked by the Loch Ness monster. The huge ugly beast easily tosses the fisherman and his boat high in the air, and opens its mouth, waiting for the fisherman to fall in. As the man flies through the air in horror, he cries out, 'Oh God! Please help me!'

All of a sudden, the man freezes in mid-air, not falling, not moving. A voice booms down from the heavens: 'I thought you did not believe in me. Why, then, do you ask for my help?'

The guy says, 'Hey, God, mate, cut me some slack. Twenty seconds ago, I didn't believe in the Loch Ness monster either.'

★★★

A faith healer is addressing his audience, convincing them of the benefits of faith and prayer as a means of curing the sick. He asks for volunteers from the audience so he can prove his powers. Two men come forward.

'What ails you, lad?' says the healer to the first man named Robbie.

'I've got a b-b-b-b-bad s-s-s-s-stammer,' is the reply.

'And you?' the healer says to Ken, the second man, who leans unsteadily on wooden crutches.

'I've been a partial cripple since birth.'

'Now,' says the healer, 'I will show you how the power of our Lord will help you overcome your illness.'

He lays one hand across Robbie's mouth, and the other on Ken's leg, and encourages his audience to pray together. He whips everyone into such a frenzy that they all believe that anything is possible. Then he says to the two men, 'Do you have faith in God, do you believe in the power?'

'YES!' says Ken.

'Y-Y-Y-YES!' says Robbie.

'Now, I want you to go behind that screen and do exactly as I say.'

So Ken and Robbie go behind the screen and the healer says, 'Ken, if you truly believe then throw out your crutches!'

To everyone's amazement, Ken's crutches come sailing over the top of the screen. Then the healer says, 'Now, Robbie, if you truly believe, say something!'.

After a hushed silence, a voice rings out, 'K-K-e-n's f-f-fallen over.'

★★★

What's the definition of a masochist?
A celibate priest. They give up their sex lives only to have people come in and tell them the highlights.

★★★

There was a Pope who was loved by all men, and when he died and went to Heaven, Saint Peter met him in a warm embrace.

'Welcome, your holiness, we are honoured to have you here. Your dedication in serving your fellow man has earned you great respect here, and for this we grant you free access to all parts of Heaven. Now, is there anything that your holiness desires?'

'Well, yes,' the Pope replied. 'I have spent many years trying to work out the mysteries of the universe. I have spent hours pondering questions that have confounded philosophers through the ages. I would dearly love to read the transcripts which recorded the actual conversations between God and the prophets of old. I would love to see what was actually said first-hand.'

Saint Peter immediately ushered the Pope to the Heavenly library. The Pope sat down and began to read the true history of the Earth. Some time later a scream of heart-chilling anguish rang out from the bookshelves of the library. Hordes of angels came running. There they found the Pope with a look of horror on his face pointing to a single world on an old parchment, repeating over and over, 'There's an "R", there's an "R" – it's "celib*r*ate!"

To Old People

Insults

You bloomin' old crumblie!

★★★

When you were young, rainbows were in black and white.

★★★

You old crackers!

★★★

You oldie.

★★★

You're so old, you'd have an autographed Bible.

★★★

When you were young, the Dead Sea was just getting sick.

★★★

You basket of wrinkles.

★★★

You're so old, you'd remember when Jesus was just a boy.

★★★

You old baked-bean fart.

★★★

You're so old, you'd remember when Moby Dick was just a tadpole.

★★★

I've seen raisins with less wrinkles.

★★★

Your birthday cake looks like a bushfire!

★★★

You're so old, you'd remember when Mr Squiggle was just a pencil.

★★★

You old elephant skin.

★★★

For you, 'getting lucky' means finding your car in the bingo car park.

★★★

You sure act your age, mate – senile.

★★★

You're so old, your birth certificate is in Roman numerals.

★★★

You're so old, you'd remember when Uluru was just a pebble.

★★★

It looks like the wrinkle-fairy tap-danced on your face.

★★★

You old cronie.

★★★

You're alive, but only in the sense that you can't be legally buried.

★★★

You've got more wrinkles than an elephant's scrotum.

★★★

You're so old, an 'all-nighter' means not getting up for a piss.

★★★

You've been pressing forty for so long it's pleated.

You're so old, when you were born your family tree was just a sapling.

When you were at school, ancient history was called current affairs.

You've got so many wrinkles, you could screw on your Akubra.

You don't have to worry about saving 'for the future'.

You'd get winded playing poker.

You're still chasing women, but can't remember why.

Your little black book contains only next-of-kin.

Jokes

Merle and Morten had been married for sixty-five years and were seeing out their twilight years in a nursing home.

One morning, Merle sweetly asked, 'Morten, love, would you like me to fetch you some breakfast?'

'Yes please, Merle,' smiled Morten. 'Could you please get me a bowl of All-Bran, a glass of orange juice and a pot of tea.'

Merle started to totter out the door and Morten called out, 'Merle, darling, shouldn't you be writing this down? You know how your memory is fading!'

'No, Morten, love, I'll remember!' she assured him.

Three hours later, Merle returns from the kitchen with a double chocolate sundae and a strawberry milkshake.

'You and your bloody memory, Merle!' chided Morten, 'I knew that you'd forget the nuts!'

★★★

Three old blokes were sitting on a park bench when a pretty jogger went past. The first old chap said, 'If I were younger I'd jump up and grab that girlie and give her a big cuddle.'

The second old bloke said, 'If I were younger I'd jump up and grab that girlie and give her a big cuddle and *then* a passionate kiss.'

The third old chap said, 'If I were younger I'd jump up and grab that girlie and give her a big cuddle and a passionate kiss, *then* I'd throw her on the ground, rip her shorts off and ... what was that other thing we used to do?'

★★★

Old Clarry was a 95-year-old larrikin. One afternoon he was a little bored, and decided to remove his dressing-gown and streak across the nursing home lawn completely naked.

'Hey girls! Like what you see?' he cackled to old Ruby and Ivy who were enjoying a cup of tea on the veranda.

'Dearie me, Ruby!' croaked Ivy. 'What on Earth was that?'

'I don't know, love,' Ruby rasped, 'but whatever it was, it could certainly do with a good ironing.'

★★★

Jesus was taking a wander through Heaven when he noticed an old man sitting on a doorstep, looking rather sadly at his shoes.

'Mate,' said Jesus, 'you're in Heaven, you should be happy! What's the problem?'

The old man continued to look down at his shoes and sighed, 'I've been looking for my son and I haven't been able to find him.'

Jesus said kindly, 'Tell me about it.'

'Well,' began the man, 'on Earth I was a carpenter, and one day my son disappeared. I never heard from him again, and I was hoping to find him here in Heaven.'

With his heart suddenly beating faster, Jesus bent over the old man and said, 'Father?'

The old man turned, looked up and cried, 'Pinocchio?'

***

Ninety-two-year-old Mavis wanders into the dayroom of the nursing home with her fist clenched. She raises it into the air and announces: 'Anyone who is able to guess what I'm holding in my hand can have sex with me tonight!'

After a long silence, one old bloke gruffly sighs, 'It's a flamin' elephant!'

Mavis raises her eyebrow suggestively and purrs, 'Close enough, sweetheart!'

★★★

When Josie married Jeremy, the love of her life, she put a shoebox in her closet and asked her husband never to touch it. For fifty years Jeremy didn't touch it. One day though, as they were packing up the house to move into a retirement village in Brisbane, he came across the box. Not being able to help himself, he opened it and found two hand-knitted doilies and $94,300 in cash.

He took the box to his wife and asked about the contents.

'My mother gave me that box the day we married,' Josie explained. 'She told me to make a doily each time I got mad at you; that it would ease my anger.'

Jeremy was very touched that in fifty years she'd only been mad at him twice. 'What's the $94,300 for?' he asked.

'Oh, that's the money I've made selling the doilies.'

★★★

Two older couples are out for a walk. The women are walking ahead of the men.

Jake says to Tim, 'We went out to a great place for dinner last night – the food and atmosphere was just great, and it didn't cost the Earth.'

Tim says, 'Yeah? Emma and I eat out a lot. What was the name?'

Jake says, 'You know, Tim, my memory isn't what it used to be. You'll have to help me out here. What's the name of that very pretty flower that smells sweet and grows on a prickly bush?'

Tim says, 'Could it be a rose?'

Jake replies, 'A rose. Yes, that's it, a rose. Hey, Rose! What was the name of that nice restaurant where we had dinner last night?'

★★★

An old codger is worried that he might be losing his memory and pays a visit to the doctor.

'Doc, I'm always forgetting my car keys, my glasses, and the other day I went out for a stroll and forgot where I lived. Last week, I forgot my wife's birthday, and then today I

forgot her name! I don't know how much
longer I can cope with this. Tell me doc, what
can I do?'

'How long have you been experiencing this
problem?' the doctor replies.

'Er ... what problem?'

When her beloved pair of pet rabbits died, the
old woman thought it'd be nice to put them
on her mantelpiece, so she took them to the
taxidermist to have them stuffed.

'I can stuff these, no worries,' said the
taxidermist. 'Do you want them mounted?'

'No,' she sighed, 'just holding hands.'

★★★

The 10 Benefits of Being Old

1. People call at 9 p.m. and ask, 'Did I wake
   you?'
2. No one expects you to run into a burning
   building.
3. People no longer view you as a
   hypochondriac – you really are sick.
4. Things you buy now won't wear out.
5. You don't have to worry about saving 'for
   the future'.
6. You can avoid crowds at restaurants by
   eating dinner at 5 p.m.

7. You enjoy hearing about other people's operations.
8. You have a party and the neighbours don't even realise it.
9. Your investment in health insurance is finally beginning to pay off.
10. Your secrets are safe with your friends because they can't remember them either.

To
Blondes

Insults

You're a blonde.
And really, that says it all!

Jokes

What is a blonde doing when she holds her hands tightly over her ears?
Trying to hold on to a thought.

What do you do when a blonde throws a pin at you?
Get the hell out of there, she's got a grenade in her mouth.

What job function does a blonde have in an
M&M factory?
Proofreading.

***

What's the first thing a blonde learns when
she has a driving lesson?
That she can also sit upright in a car.

***

What is the difference between a blonde and
the Grand Old Duke of York?
*The Grand Old Duke of York only had 10,000
men.*

***

What happened to the blonde tap dancer?
She slipped off and fell down the drain.

***

What's black and fuzzy and hangs from the ceiling?
A blonde electrician.

★★★

Why did the blonde fail her driver's licence test?
She wasn't used to the front seat.

★★★

What's the difference between a blonde and a shopping trolley?
The shopping trolley has a mind of its own.

★★★

What's the difference between blondes and traffic signs?
Some traffic signs say 'stop'.

★★★

Why do blondes wear earmuffs?
To avoid the draft.

★★★

What does a blonde say after multiple orgasms?
'Way to go, team!'

★★★

Why do blondes wear underpants?
To keep their ankles warm.

★★★

Why do blondes get confused in the ladies'
room?
They have to pull their own pants down.

A blonde came out of the kitchen distraught.
'Honey!' she cried to her boyfriend, 'I was just
rinsing some ice cubes and now they've
disappeared!'

What do intelligent blondes and UFOs have in
common?
*They're often talked about, but no one knows if
they exist.*

Why should you never take a blonde out for
coffee?
It's too hard to re-train them.

What's the difference between a blonde and
an ironing board?
*It's difficult to open the legs of an ironing
board.*

How do you plant dope?
Bury a blonde.

What's the mating call of the blonde?
'I'm so drunk!'

★★★

What's another mating call of the blonde?
'Next!'

★★★

What does the postcard from a blonde's
holiday say?
Having a wonderful time. Where am I?

★★★

Why do blondes drive cars with sunroofs?
More leg room.

★★★

Why did the blonde stare at a bottle of orange
juice for two hours?
It said 'concentrate'.

★★★

Why did the blonde put her finger over the
nail she was hammering?
The noise gave her a headache.

★★★

Why did the blonde climb up to the roof of
the bar?
She heard that the drinks were on the house.

★★★

Why do blondes work seven days a week?
So you don't have to retrain them on Monday.

★★★

What's the definition of a metallurgist?
A man who can tell if a platinum blonde is a virgin metal or a common ore.

★★★

What's the difference between Elvis and a smart blonde?
Elvis has been sighted.

★★★

What's the difference between a blonde and a light bulb?
The light bulb is smarter, but the blonde is easier to turn on.

★★★

What's the difference between a blonde and a brick?
When you lay a brick it doesn't follow you around for two weeks whining.

★★★

What is foreplay for a blonde?
Thirty minutes of begging.

★★★

Why don't blondes make good pharmacists?
They can't get the bottle into the typewriter.

★★★

What did the blonde do when her doctor told her she had sugar in her urine?
She peed on her Special K.

★★★

Why don't blondes call 000 in an emergency?
They can't remember the number.

★★★

Celebrant to a blonde: 'Do you take this man to be your lawful wedded husband, in good times or in bad?'
The blonde replied, 'In good times.'

★★★

Why don't blondes eat jelly?
They can't figure out how to get two cups of water into those little packages.

★★★

How does a blonde commit suicide?
She gathers her clothes into a pile and jumps off.

★★★

Why did God give blondes more brains than horses?
Because he didn't want them shitting in the streets during parades.

★★★

How do you get a one-armed blonde out of a tree?
Wave to her.

★★★

How does a blonde measure her IQ?
With a tyre gauge.

★★★

How does a blonde turn on the light after she has had sex?
She opens the car door.

★★★

How do you get a blonde's eyes to twinkle?
Shine a torch in her ears.

★★★

How do you tell when a blonde reaches orgasm?
The next person in the queue taps you on the shoulder.

★★★

How do you describe a blonde surrounded by drooling idiots?
Flattered.

★★★

Why do blondes shower in the kitchen sink?
Because that's where you're supposed to wash vegetables.

★★★

Why don't blondes eat bananas?
They can't find the zipper.

★★★

Why don't blondes eat pickles?
Because they can't get their head in the jar.

★★★

What is the worst thing about sex with a blonde?
Bucket seats.

★★★

What important question does a blonde ask her mate before having sex?
'Do you want this by the hour or the flat rate?'

★★★

How many blondes does it take to change a light bulb?
Two. One to hold the Diet Coke, and one to call, 'Daddy!'

★★★

What's the difference between a blonde and a Porsche?
You don't lend the Porsche out to your mates.

★★★

What do you call a blonde with a balloon on her shoulder?
Siamese twins.

★★★

What is the difference between butter and a blonde?
Butter is difficult to spread.

How do you get a blonde to say "Ouch!"?
Phone her while she's ironing.

How do you get a blonde to say "Ouch!" twice?
Phone her again while she's ironing.

What is the difference between a blonde and the *Titanic?*
They know how many men went down on the Titanic.

What do you say to a blonde feminist with no arms and no legs?
'Nice tits!'

What does a blonde make best for dinner?
Reservations.

What do blondes and cow pats have in common?
They both get easier to pick up with age.

★★★

What does a blonde say when you ask her if her blinker is on?
It's on. It's off. It's on. It's off. It's on. It's off.

★★★

What do you get when you offer a blonde a penny for her thoughts?
Change.

★★★

Why do blondes wear ponytails?
To hide the air-valve.

★★★

How can you tell that a blonde has a boyfriend?
There's a buckle-print on her forehead.

★★★

What do you call a skeleton in the closet with blonde hair?
Last year's hide-and-seek winner.

★★★

What do you call a basement full of blondes?
A whine cellar.

★★★

What do you call five blondes at the bottom of the pool?
Air bubbles.

★★★

What do you call a blonde lesbian?
A waste.

★★★

What do you call four blondes lying on the ground?
An air mattress.

★★★

What do you call a dumb blonde behind a steering wheel?
An air bag.

★★★

What do you call a blonde between two brunettes?
A mental block.

★★★

What do you call ten blondes standing ear to ear?
A wind tunnel.

★★★

What do you call fifteen blondes in a circle?
A dope ring.

★★★

What do you call an unmarried blonde in a BMW?
A divorcee.

★★★

What do you call a blonde with two brain cells?
Pregnant.

★★★

What do you call a blonde at university?
A visitor.

★★★

What do you call a brunette with a blonde on either side?
An interpreter.

★★★

What do you call a blonde in a tree with a brief case?
A branch manager.

★★★

What do you see when you look into a blonde's eyes?
The back of her head.

★★★

What do a blonde and your computer have in common?
You don't know how much either of them mean to you until they go down on you.

★★★

What do a blonde and a beer bottle have in common?
They're both empty from the neck up.

★★★

Why did the blonde cross the road?
Never mind that! What was she doing outside of the bedroom?

★★★

Why did the blonde scale the chain-link fence?
To see what was on the other side.

★★★

Why didn't the blonde want a window-seat on the plane?
She'd just blow-dried her hair and she didn't want it blown around too much.

★★★

What's the difference between a chorus line of blondes and a magician?
A magician has a cunning array of stunts.

★★★

What is the best blonde secretary in the world to have?
One that never misses a period.

What does a blonde think an innuendo is?
An Italian suppository.

★★★

What can save a dying blonde?
Hair transplants.

★★★

What did the blonde think of the new computer?
She didn't like it because she couldn't get MTV.

★★★

What does a blonde say during a porno?
'There I am!'

★★★

How do you make a blonde laugh on a Monday morning?
Tell her a joke on Friday night.

★★★

How do you confuse a blonde?
You don't. They're born that way.

★★★

Do you know why the blonde got fired from
the M&M factory?
She threw out all the Ws.

★★★

Why does a blonde have fur on her
underpants?
To keep her ankles warm.

★★★

How can you tell if a blonde has a vibrator?
By the chipped tooth.

★★★

How do you keep a blonde busy?
*Write 'Please turn over' on both sides of a piece
of paper.*

★★★

Why do blondes wear shoulder-pads?
To keep from bruising their ears.

★★★

What does a blonde answer to the question:
'Are you sexually active?'
'No, I just lie there.'

★★★

What's the first thing a blonde says in the morning?
'Thanks, guys ...'

★★★

What's brown and red and black and blue?
A brunette who has told one too many blonde jokes.

★★★

What's the difference between a blonde and a Mallee bull?
The blonde has the higher sperm count.

★★★

What's the difference between a crazy fighting hockey player and a blonde?
He is fussy by nature and would go to any length to get a puck.

★★★

Why does a blonde only change her baby's nappies every month?
Because it says on the packet, 'good for up to 10 kilograms.'

★★★

How does a blonde spell 'farm'?
E-I-E-I-O.

★★★

Why do blondes have see-through lunchbox
lids?
*So that when they're on the train they can tell if
they're going to work or coming home.*

★★★

Why do blondes have TGIF on their shoes?
Toes go in first.

★★★

Why do blondes have TGIF on their shirts?
Tits go in front.

clever!

TGIF

★★★

What do you say to a blonde that won't give in?
'Have another beer.'

★★★

What do peroxide blondes and black men have in common?
They both have black roots.

★★★

What does a blonde owl say?
'What, what?'

★★★

Why did the blonde have tread-marks on her back?
From crawling across the street when the sign said 'DON'T WALK.'

★★★

Why did the blonde tiptoe past the medicine cabinet?
So she wouldn't wake up the sleeping pills.

★★★

Why did God create blondes?
Because kangaroos can't bring beer from the fridge.

Okay, why did God create brunettes?
Neither could the blondes.

Why did the blonde wear condoms on her ears?
So she wouldn't get hearing aides.

Why did the blonde drive into the ditch?
To turn the blinker off.

Why did the blonde snort Nutrasweet?
She thought it was Diet Coke.

What is blonde, brunette, blonde, brunette?
A nude blonde doing cartwheels.

What is the difference between a blonde and an inflatable doll?
About two cans of hairspray.

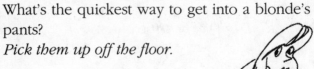

***

What's the quickest way to get into a blonde's pants?
Pick them up off the floor.

***

Where do blondes go to meet their relatives?
The vegetable garden.

***

How many blondes does it take to play tag?
One.

What did the blonde name her pet zebra?
Spot.

★★★

Why can't blondes put in light bulbs?
They keep breaking them with the hammers.

★★★

Did you hear about the blonde rabbit?
She got stuck in a trap, chewed off three legs and was still stuck.

★★★

Why was the blonde upset when she got her driver's licence?
Because she got an 'F' in sex.

★★★

Did you hear about the blonde who shot an arrow into the air?
She missed.

★★★

Why is a blonde like a doorknob?
Because everybody gets a turn.

★★★

What's a blonde's favourite nursery rhyme?
Humpme Dumpme.

★★★

Why can't blondes be jillaroos on a cattle
station?
They can't keep their calves together.

***

What did the blonde customer say to the
buxom waitress (after reading her nametag)?
*'Janie ... that's cute. So what did you name the
other boob?'*

***

Why is a blonde like railway tracks?
Because she's been laid all over the country.

***

What does a blonde do if she is not in bed by
10 p.m.?
She picks up her purse and goes home.

★★★

What does a blonde consider long and hard?
Kindergarten.

★★★

What is the definition of the perfect woman?
*A deaf and dumb blonde nymphomaniac
whose father owns a pub.*

★★★

What's a blonde's idea of safe sex?
Locking the car door.

★★★

Why did the blonde keep failing her driver's
test?
*Because every time the door opened, she
jumped into the back seat.*

★★★

What did the blonde do when she heard that
almost all accidents occur around the home?
She moved.

★★★

Did you hear about the blonde who tried to blow up her husband's car?
She burned her lips on the exhaust pipe.

★★★

How do blonde brain-cells die?
Alone.

★★★

How do you keep a blonde busy all day long?
Put her in a round room and tell her to sit in the corner.

★★★

How do you get a blonde to marry you?
Tell her she's pregnant.

★★★

A blonde bought a book at the local bookshop called *Flight to France*. She got back home and found out it was volume four of the encyclopaedia.

★★★

A blonde started her first day at her new school with a pair of headphones on. Her teacher, realising how difficult it was starting a new school, did not want to embarrass the girl so said nothing. But the next day, and the next day again, the blonde continued to wear the headphones. Finally, the teacher asked her to take the headphones off. The blonde refused.

He let the issue rest for a while, but as another week went on and she was still wearing the headphones, he called her aside after class and demanded that she remove them. She looked at him sullenly and said nothing. Exasperated, he ripped them off, whereupon she immediately fell to the floor, dead.

After the ambulance had taken her body away, he picked up the headphones to see what she had been listening to. He put them on and heard, 'Breathe in ... breathe out ... breathe in ... breathe out ...'

★★★

The blonde's husband said his wife was obsessed with shopping.

'She's mad, she'll buy anything that's marked down. Yesterday she came home with an escalator.'

★★★

A blonde was suffering from constipation, so her doctor prescribed suppositories. A week later she went back to the doctor, still suffering the same problem.

'Have you been taking them regularly?' asked the doctor.

'What do you think I've been doing,' replied the blonde. 'Shoving them up my arse?'

***

A scantily clad blonde is sitting in a bar. Having never shaved in her life, she has a thick black bush of hair in each armpit. She chugs down drinks like a man and every ten minutes she raises her arm and flags the bartender for another bourbon. Each time she flags the bartender, the other drinkers in the bar are given an eyeful of her hairy pits. After a few hours, a drunk at the other end of the bar says to the bartender, 'Hey, I'd like to buy Miss Ballerina here a drink.'
The bartender replies, 'She's not a ballerina. What makes you think she's a ballerina?' The drunk says, 'Any girl that can lift her leg that high has to be a ballerina!'

***

Two blondes were walking along the train tracks one morning after spending all night at the pub.

'Wow, these stairs are killing me,' said the first blonde.

The second blonde groaned back, 'The stairs don't bother me as much as the low handrail.'

★★★

A blonde needed to send a message to her mother who was overseas. She went into the communications centre, but was told it would cost $50.

She said, 'I'm desperate to talk to Mum, but I don't have any money. Please, I'll do anything for you if you would help me!'

The man arched an eyebrow, 'Anything?' he leered.

'Yes, anything,' promised the blonde.

So the man took her into a room down the hall and shut the door.

Then he said, 'Get down on your knees.'

She did.

Then he said, 'Undo my zipper.'

She did.

Then he said, 'Now take out my willy.'

She took it out and grabbed hold of it with both hands.

The man closed his eyes, and whispered, 'Go for it.'

The blonde slowly brought her mouth closer to his willy, and while holding it close to her lips, she said, 'Hello, Mum?'

★★★

Two blondes are walking through the woods. One looks down and says, 'Hey, look at the deer tracks.'
The other blonde takes a closer look and says, 'Those aren't deer tracks, they're bear tracks, silly!'
The two argue back and forth about which animal's tracks they are, until ten minutes later when they are hit by a train.

★★★

Tired of being called dumb by everyone she knew, a blonde spent weeks and weeks learning all the capitals for every state of Australia. She was out shopping one day when she passed a group of guys and heard one of them telling a blonde joke. She turned around and said to them indignantly, 'Hey, not all blondes are stupid, you know. Let me prove it. Tell me the name of any state in Australia and I'll tell you it's capital.' 'Victoria,' suggested one of the guys.
'And the capital of Victoria is "V",' was her triumphant response.

Insults For Any Occasion

Go and take a running jump at yourself.

***

Go dip your eye in hot cocky cack.

***

I hope all your chooks turn into emus and knock your dunny door down.

***

You're a nasty piece of bacon gristle.

***

I'll knock your teeth so far down your throat you'll have to stick a toothbrush up your arse to clean them.

***

You'd bore the hair off a gay man's moustache.

***

Pull your head in.

***

Put a sock in it.

★★★

You're the scum of the Earth.

★★★

You're as nervous as a mother roo in a room full of pickpockets.

★★★

You're a slime ball.

★★★

Put a cork in it.

★★★

What the bloody hell's crawlin' on you, mate?

★★★

You whacker.

★★★

Go bite your bum.

★★★

You're an arsehole.

★★★

You scunge bag.

★★★

You're a nasty piece of work.

***

You arse-licker.

***

You're a crawler.

***

You're a brown-noser.

***

You shiny arse.

***

You grizzleguts.

***

You're as clumsy as a duck in a ploughed paddock.

***

If bullshit was music you'd be a concerto.

***

If bullshit was snow you'd be a blizzard.

★★★

You're a hoon.

★★★

You're a dingo.

★★★

I wouldn't jump on you if you were a trampoline.

★★★

You're as low as shark bait.

★★★

You're lower than a snake's belly.

★★★

You're a scumbag.

★★★

I wouldn't piss on you if you were on fire.

★★★

You'd make a blowfly sick.

★★★

You look like a stunned mullet.

★★★

You give me the Jimmy Brits. (Rhyming slang for 'You give me the shits'.)

★★★

You're lower than shark shit.

★★★

You're a suck.

★★★

You're nosy enough to want to know the ins and outs of a chook's bum.

★★★

Up your arse with a piece of glass.

★★★

I wouldn't piss down your throat if your guts were on fire.

★★★

You're as popular as a pork chop in a synagogue.

★★★

You're as high as a dingo's howl (foul-smelling).

★★★

You couldn't lie straight in bed.

★★★

You're as rough as hessian bags.

★★★

You're as rough as guts.

★★★

You could talk under water with a mouthful of marbles.

★★★

You could talk under wet cement with a mouthful of marbles.

★★★

I wouldn't use you for ammo in a shit fight.

★★★

You've got tickets on yourself.

★★★

You're nothing out of the box.

★★★

You're a no-hoper.

★★★

You've got more front than David Jones (ritzy department store).

★★★

You're up yourself.

★★★

If dung was dirt you'd cover an acre.

★★★